Bloom's
GUIDES

Lorraine Hansberry's
A Raisin in the Sun

The Adventures of
  Huckleberry Finn
All the Pretty Horses
Animal Farm
The Autobiography of Malcolm X
The Awakening
The Bell Jar
Beloved
Beowulf
Brave New World
The Canterbury Tales
Catch-22
The Catcher in the Rye
The Chosen
The Crucible
Cry, the Beloved Country
Death of a Salesman
Fahrenheit 451
Frankenstein
The Glass Menagerie
The Grapes of Wrath
Great Expectations
The Great Gatsby
Hamlet
The Handmaid's Tale
Heart of Darkness
The House on Mango Street
I Know Why the Caged Bird Sings
The Iliad
Invisible Man
Jane Eyre

The Kite Runner
Lord of the Flies
Macbeth
Maggie: A Girl of the Streets
The Member of the Wedding
The Metamorphosis
Native Son
Night
1984
The Odyssey
Oedipus Rex
Of Mice and Men
One Hundred Years of Solitude
Pride and Prejudice
Ragtime
A Raisin in the Sun
The Red Badge of Courage
Romeo and Juliet
The Scarlet Letter
A Separate Peace
Slaughterhouse-Five
Snow Falling on Cedars
The Stranger
A Streetcar Named Desire
The Sun Also Rises
A Tale of Two Cities
The Things They Carried
To Kill a Mockingbird
Uncle Tom's Cabin
The Waste Land
Wuthering Heights

Bloom's
GUIDES

Lorraine Hansberry's
A Raisin in the Sun

Edited & with an Introduction
by Harold Bloom

BLOOM'S
LITERARY CRITICISM
An imprint of Infobase Publishing

Bloom's Guides: A Raisin in the Sun

Copyright © 2009 by Infobase Publishing

Introduction © 2009 by Harold Bloom

Bloom's Literary Criticism
An imprint of Infobase Publishing
132 West 31st Street
New York, NY 10001

Library of Congress Cataloging-in-Publication Data
Lorraine Hansberry's A raisin in the sun / edited and with an introduction by Harold Bloom.
    p. cm. — (Bloom's guides)
  Includes bibliographical references and index.
  ISBN 978-1-60413-202-1 (acid-free paper) 1. Hansberry, Lorraine, 1930–1965. Raisin in the sun. 2. Domestic drama, American—History and criticism. 3. African American families in literature. I. Bloom, Harold. II. Title. III. Series.
  PS3515.A515R3375 2008
  812'.54—dc22
                                            2008033184

Contributing Editor: Amy Sickels
Cover design by Takeshi Takahashi
Printed in the United States of America
Bang EJB 10 9 8 7 6 5 4 3 2 1
This book is printed on acid-free paper.

Contents

Introduction

HAROLD BLOOM

I saw *A Raisin in the Sun* almost exactly half a century ago in its New Haven tryout and remember that it seemed effective theater. Until just now I had not read the play and have never attended a revival of it nor seen the film versions. Reading *Raisin* necessarily is a mixed experience. Like most successful American dramas it performs better than it reads, which hardly is an assault on a poignant historical and social text. Alas, I regret to say that now in 2008 with Obama fighting a campaign for the American presidency, a breakthrough theatrical event of 1958–59 sadly qualifies as a period piece and not, I think, as a permanent work of American dramatic literature.

Hansberry was a civil rights and women's rights pioneer and a forerunner also of the struggle for lesbian vindication in American society. Of the principal modern American playwrights, she has something more in common with Arthur Miller than she does with O'Neill, Williams, Wilder, Albee, Mamet, and Kushner. She lacks however the rough eloquence that Miller, at his rare best, brought to social theater.

The aesthetic judgment on any play cannot be compounded of politics and history but must turn at last on the quality of language, the power of thought, the persuasiveness of characterization. By those standards, the dramas of Hansberry are dignified exemplars of a particular decade in our sociopolitical history. Reading *A Raisin in the Sun* and *The Sign in Sidney Brustein's Window* is a difficult experience in 2008. As there are no realized personalities among the characters, no eloquence in the language, and only worn-out clichés in the dramatist's stance and attitude, it becomes impossible to sustain a suspension of critical judgment. Hansberry deserved all honor for her courage and foresight, much in advance of her time.

Biographical Sketch

Lorraine Hansberry was born on May 19, 1930, in Chicago, Illinois, the youngest of four children of Carl Augustus Hansberry and Nannie Perry Hansberry. Her father was a prominent real estate broker and a member of the Republican Party. He generously supported African-American causes and ran for Congress. Hansberry's parents were intellectuals and activists, and their home was often visited by famous African Americans, such as Paul Robeson and W.E.B. Du Bois.

Hansberry grew up in a middle-class family. They lived on the South Side of Chicago in the Woodlawn neighborhood; then, when Lorraine was eight years old, the family moved to an all-white neighborhood and Hansberry attended a predominately white public school. The family faced intense racial discrimination, and her father engaged in a legal battle against a racially restrictive covenant that attempted to prohibit African-American families from buying homes in particular neighborhoods. The legal struggle led to the landmark Supreme Court case of *Hansberry* v. *Lee, 311 U.S. 32* (1940). The Hansberry family was victorious but still subject to living in a hostile white neighborhood; unfortunately, the ruling did little to change Chicago's segregated housing patterns and practices.

After high school, Hansberry attended the University of Wisconsin-Madison for two years. She also took courses at Roosevelt College in Chicago and the University of Guadalajara in Mexico. At Madison, she attended a school performance of *Juno and the Paycock* by the Irish playwright Sean O'Casey. The drama, about the struggles of a poor urban family in Dublin, left a strong impression on her. She decided to become a writer.

In 1950, she dropped out of college and moved to New York City. She lived in Greenwich Village and took writing classes at the New School for Social Research and worked as an associate editor of Paul Robeson's *Freedom* newspaper. During this period, she met the esteemed writer Langston Hughes and other notable African Americans. When she was completing a seminar on African history, taught by W.E.B. Du Bois, she wrote a research paper titled "The Belgian Congo: A Preliminary Report on Its Land, Its History and Its People." Hansberry became involved in a number of liberal causes. In 1952, she attended the Intercontinental Peace Congress in Uruguay as a substitute for Paul Robeson, who could not get a passport from the U.S. State Department. The following year, Hansberry married Robert Nemiroff, a Jewish literature student and songwriter she met on a picket line protesting discrimination at New York University. Hansberry worked various jobs, including waitress, typist, and cashier.

Hansberry finished writing *A Raisin in the Sun* in 1957. The production first ran in New Haven, Philadelphia, and Chicago. On March 11, 1959, it opened at the Ethel Barrymore Theatre in New York City, where it ran for 530 performances. It was the first play to be produced on Broadway that was written and directed by an African American and had an all-black cast. The original production, directed by Lloyd Richards, starred Sidney Poitier, Ruby Dee, and Claudia McNeil. The actor Ossie Davis eventually replaced Poitier. In 1959, the New York Drama Critics' Circle voted *A Raisin in the Sun* best American play. Hansberry was the youngest American, the fifth woman, and the first African American to win the prestigious award. In 1961, the play was adapted into a successful film, starring Sidney Poitier, with the script written by Hansberry.

The success of *A Raisin in the Sun* gave Hansberry a chance to become a more influential voice in the American civil rights movement and the African struggle to free itself from European colonial rule. She helped raise money, gave speeches, and took part in panels and interviews, speaking at civil rights rallies and writers' conferences. She wrote more than 60 magazine and newspaper articles, poems, speeches, and the text of *The Movement: Documentary of a Struggle for Equality*, a photographic essay on the civil rights movement. In 1963, she left her hospital bed to give a talk to the winners of the United Negro College Fund writing contest, in which she used the phrase "To be young, gifted, and Black," which later became the title of her autobiography, a collection of her assorted writings. Although Hansberry never openly declared her sexual orientation, she wrote a pseudo-anonymous letter to *The Ladder*, one of the first lesbian publications in the United States. In 1964, Nemiroff and Hansberry divorced.

Hansberry's other writings include *The Drinking Gourd* (1959), which focuses on the American slavery system. The story had been commissioned for the National Broadcasting Company but was not produced because it was considered too controversial for television. Her next play, *The Sign in Sidney Brustein's Window* (1964), received mixed reviews and was moderately successful on Broadway, opening and closing in 1965. The play, with only one black character, concerns a Jewish intellectual who works on the campaign of a local politician and becomes disillusioned. By the time it opened, Hansberry was already spending much of her time in the hospital. She started to write the play *Les Blancs* in 1960. Unfortunately, she would not live to see it produced. Hansberry died of pancreatic cancer on January 12, 1965, at the age of 34.

After her death, Nemiroff adapted Hansberry's writings as the play *To Be Young, Gifted, and Black*, which was produced off-Broadway in 1969; it was published as a book the following year. *Les Blancs*, a drama set in Africa, was also adapted by Nemiroff and first presented by Konrad Matthaei at the Longacre Theatre, in New York City, in 1970. In 1973, Nemiroff and Charlotte Zaltzberg adapted *A Raisin in the Sun* into a musical, titled *Raisin*. It won the Tony Award for best musical in 1974 and ran on Broadway for nearly three years. Lorraine Hansberry's premature death cut short her promising career. Although her reputation grew with various posthumous publications, she remains best known for *A Raisin in the Sun*.

The Story Behind the Story

In 1959, *A Raisin in the Sun* made Lorraine Hansberry the youngest American and the first black playwright to win the Best Play of the Year Award of the New York Drama Critics's Circle. She was twenty-nine years old. The play was subsequently published in more than 30 languages and produced worldwide. It quickly became an American classic, and her unprecedented success opened the floodgates for a new generation of black actors and writers.

Nobody expected this kind of success. Because Hansberry was an African-American woman, as well as a new playwright, it was difficult to find support on Broadway. The producer, Phil Rose, had never mounted a play before, and it took eighteen months to find a co-producer, with nearly every established producer turning him down. Finally, he was joined by David Cogan, another newcomer to the business. Once they had the money, not a single theater in New York would rent to them. The play was moved to New Haven, Philadelphia, and Chicago, where it received critical and popular support. It opened on Broadway at the Ethel Barrymore Theatre on March 11, 1959, where it was an enormous success, running for 530 performances. The stellar cast included Sidney Poitier in the lead role of Walter Lee, Ruby Dee as Ruth, Claudia McNeil as Mama Younger, and Diana Sands as Beneatha.

When the play was produced in 1959, several cuts were made. The long running time was a concern, and some of the cuts helped strengthen the play. But other cuts affected specific racial themes, altering the way the play was interpreted. For example, the scene in which Beneatha displays her natural haircut was taken out, removing Hansberry's point about the beauty of natural black hair. Mrs. Johnson's visit, which adds about ten minutes to the play, did not appear in the first production and even now is rarely included. However, this important scene reveals the violence the Youngers may face by moving to a white neighborhood. Another scene that was cut depicted Travis chasing the rat, an example of the horrible conditions of ghetto life.

Many early reviews praised the play for its universal themes, stressing that the Younger family could have been any American family, including a middle-class white family. Hansberry was thrilled by the supportive reviews and positive critical response but also felt troubled by the various misunderstandings of the play that also emerged. She insisted that her play was essentially about an African-American family in a particular time and place and restored some of the cuts in the 1959 Random House edition.

A Raisin in the Sun predated the explosive revolution in the black and feminist movements and was one of the major literary catalysts of the Black Arts Movement of the 1960s. Ironically, during the height of the movement, many African-American artists objected to the play, viewing it as conservative and assimilationist. Years later, Amari Baraka explained, "We thought Hansberry's play was part of the 'passive resistance' phase of the movement" and realized later, "We missed the essence of the work—that Hansberry had created a family on the cutting edge of the same class and ideological struggles as existed in the movement itself and among the people." He now sees the play as "the accurate telling and stunning vision of the real struggle" (19).

Some of the material in the play came from Hansberry's personal life. When she was a child, her family moved from the Chicago projects to a white neighborhood. They faced intense racism, and their home was attacked by a mob, with someone hurling a brick through the window and narrowly missing eight-year-old Lorraine. Her father waged a legal battle to desegregate the white neighborhoods and was victorious in the landmark Supreme Court case of *Hansberry* v. *Lee, 311 U.S. 32* (1940). Years later, in college, Hansberry saw a performance of Sean O'Casey's *Juno and the Paycock*, about the struggles of a poor Irish family, and she knew then that she wanted to tell a similar realistic story about the oppression of African Americans. An outspoken social activist, Hansberry proudly declared, "I was born black and female," rejecting the limits society placed on her race and gender. She addressed many of the issues that she felt strongly about in *A Raisin in the Sun*, including racism, feminism, Africanism, abortion, and assimilation.

A Raisin in the Sun is considered a classic, and its reputation has continued to grow after the first Broadway production. In 1961, the play became a popular film starring one of the original cast members, Sidney Poitier; Hansberry's film adaptation won a Cannes Festival Award and was nominated for best screenplay. In 1974, the play was adapted into a Tony Award–winning musical, and in the 1980s a major resurgence began with revivals being mounted at many regional theaters. In 1989, the American Playhouse produced the complete play, unabridged for the first time, for television. *A Raisin in the Sun* has since undergone many revivals, including a well-publicized 2004 production on Broadway, starring Phylicia Rashad and Sean "Diddy" Combs.

List of Characters

Walter Lee Younger, 35, is a chauffeur who dreams of a better life. Walter wants to invest his father's life insurance money in a liquor store. He believes that financial independence will bring freedom and make him a better man. Walter spends most of the play obsessed with money; by the end, however, he regains his pride and integrity.

Lena Younger (Mama) is the matriarch of the family. She is religious, maternal, and sometimes overbearing and controlling. All of her actions stem from her unwavering, deep love for her family, and she wants to use her husband's insurance money to buy the family a house. It is her dream for her family to stay together and to see them become secure and hopeful.

Beneatha Younger dreams of going to medical school. She attends college and is an intellectual. Beneatha is an outspoken feminist, and some of her beliefs cause tension with Mama. She struggles to find her place in the world as a well-educated black woman.

Ruth Younger, Walter's wife, is the peacemaker of the family. Poverty and the problems between her and Walter exhaust her energies. She falls somewhere between the traditional Mama and the progressive Beneatha. Her pragmatism and emotional strength are revealed when she learns of the possibility of moving into a house.

Travis Younger is Walter and Ruth's ten-year-old son. Travis has no bedroom and sleeps on the living-room sofa. He is a likeable, sweet child who is spoiled by Mama.

Joseph Asagai is one of Beneatha's suitors: well mannered, good looking, and well liked. An intellectual and activist, Asagai is from Nigeria and is proud of his African heritage. Beneatha looks to him to increase her understanding of Africa.

He proposes marriage to Beneatha and wants her to return to Nigeria with him.

George Murchison is another of Beneatha's suitors. A college student, he comes from a wealthy upper-class family. The Youngers approve of him, but Beneatha dislikes his willingness to assimilate to white culture at the expense of his African heritage. He is arrogant and condescending.

Karl Lindner, the only white character in the play, arrives at the Youngers' apartment from the Clybourne Park Improvement Association. He offers them a significant amount of money to not move into the all-white neighborhood. He is a weak, ineffectual, dishonest presence in the play.

Bobo is an easily frightened, nervous man. He appears in act II, scene 3 to deliver the bad news about Willy Harris.

Willy Harris never appears onstage, but he is a source of tension in the play and a part of the unfolding action. He convinces Walter to invest in a liquor store, then runs off with the money.

Summary and Analysis

1.

Lorraine Hansberry's *A Raisin in the Sun* is a portrait of a working-class African-American family living on the South Side of Chicago in the 1950s. The main plot concerns how the Younger family will spend a $10,000 life insurance check, but the drama extends far beyond this action, as the play examines the deferred dreams of black America, the struggle for identity, and the meanings of family, home, and freedom. Within a domestic setting, the drama addresses issues of assimilation, feminism, racism, Africanism, masculinity, and class. Ahead of its time in many ways, *A Raisin in the Sun* was one of the first American plays to portray racial pride, as well as feminism, through the eyes of African Americans.

A Raisin in the Sun has been embraced both for its universal themes and for its specific depiction of the struggles of an African-American family living in racially volatile 1950s Chicago. It has been praised for its portrait of the basic human struggle to find dignity and for being one of the first plays to represent black life in an authentic way. Furthermore, the play dramatizes essential political issues about race. Poet and critic Amiri Baraka attests to the play's importance to the African-American community: "When *Raisin* first appeared in 1959, the Civil Rights Movement was in its earlier stages. And as a document reflecting the *essence* of those struggles, the play is unexcelled. For many of us it was—and remains—the quintessential civil rights drama" (10).

The play follows the struggles and frustrations of a single family in pursuit of the American Dream. In the 1950s, this pursuit typically involved owning a house with a yard and a big car; to be part of a happy, perfect family; and to be successful. Collectively, it was a packaged dream that was born of and often associated with white, suburban, middle-class culture. The Youngers, urban African Americans living in subsidized housing, are alienated from this dominant culture; critic Lloyd W. Brown argues that because the Youngers are black and poor, they are outsiders: "their deprivations expose the gap between the American dream and the Black American reality" (241). Hansberry examines the economic and social effects of racism on the members of the Younger family, as they strive to attain this ubiquitous, mythical American Dream.

The play's epigraph is a line from "Montage of a Dream Deferred" by the Harlem Renaissance poet Langston Hughes; this poem is also the source of the play's title:

What happens to a dream deferred?

Does it dry up
like a raisin in the sun?

Or fester like a sore—
and then run?

Does it stink like rotten meat?
Or crust and sugar over—
like a syrupy sweet?

Maybe it just sags
like a heavy load

Or does it just explode?

The poem considers whether people simply surrender to circumstances when their aspirations are destroyed, or if those dreams retain their power and emerge in different, unpredictable ways. Through each of the main characters, Hansberry examines how the dreams of black America have been altered, unrealized, or deferred.

Each of the main characters possesses a dream, and each family member hopes to improve the family's situation. Walter Younger desires wealth and social standing, and, more than any of the other characters, he believes that the attainment of the American Dream will bring happiness and meaning to his life. Beneatha aspires to go to medical school to become a doctor. Ruth and Lena entertain similar notions; they want to live in a nice house, which they hope will bring stability and happiness to the family. In the beginning, the characters' dreams center on the insurance check, but by the end, family, identity, and dignity emerge as more important than money. *A Raisin in the Sun* is a realistic play about racism and economic oppression, but it is also a hopeful celebration of the black American family.

The play is a realistic drama, and, with all of the action occurring inside the apartment, with domestic props such as an ironing board, it is an example of "kitchen sink" realism. The four adult family members are fully developed and sympathetic, but it is Mama and Walter who emerge as dual protagonists. The tone of *Raisin* is often somber, but Hansberry skillfully uses humor to bring the audience closer to this family. Structured as three conventional acts with distinct scenes, tension builds until the climax in **act III**. **Act I** establishes the main characters, depicting their anticipation of the insurance check's arrival. By the end of the first scene, the audience is apprised of the general focus of the play, with the dramatic tension quickly rising to the surface. In **act II**, the characters prepare to move into their new home in a white neighborhood. Their dreams are shattered when Walter loses the insurance money in a scam. **Act III** follows the aftermath of this conflict, with a climactic scene in which Walter must make a major decision and family members must rise above their difficult struggles.

2.

The play opens one morning at the Youngers' cramped South Side Chicago apartment, which is representative of its inhabitants, a place in which the furnishings "clearly had to accommodate the living of too many people for too many years—and they are tired." Though the furnishings at one time were "selected with care and love and even hope," the newness has faded: "Weariness has, in fact, won in this room." The apartment is small, with two bedrooms, one for Mama and Beneatha, and one for Walter and Ruth. Travis, Walter and Ruth's ten-year-old son, sleeps on a couch in the living room.

The only window is in the small kitchen, and the family shares a bathroom in the hall with their neighbors, the Johnsons.

Ruth is the first one to appear onstage. Similar to the surroundings, Ruth, only 30 years old, is weary and overworked, a woman who once had beauty, potential, and hope but has since been worn down: "life has been little that she expected, and disappointment has already begun to hang in her face." After she wakes Travis, encouraging him to get to the bathroom before it is occupied by the neighbors, she wakes her husband.

Walter, 35, is "a lean, intense young man" who is "inclined to quick nervous movements and erratic speech habits—and always in his voice there is a quality of indictment." Within a few lines of dialogue, Walter refers to the check and mentions a newspaper story about a bomb. At this moment, the audience may fail to understand the exact significance of these comments but trusts that Hansberry is setting up the major conflicts: the concern over money and the kind of resistance and violence the family will face in trying to attain its dreams.

The tension between Ruth and Walter is apparent immediately. Ruth is irritated with Walter for entertaining his friends the night before in the living room that serves as Travis's bedroom. Walter attempts to defuse her anger, commenting on her good looks, but Ruth is indifferent. He continues, "You looked real young again. . . . It's gone now—you look like yourself again!" insinuating that Ruth looks too old for her age. The focus quickly returns to money troubles when Travis asks for an extra fifty cents for school. Ruth refuses, saying they do not have the money, but Walter responds, "Why you tell the boy things like that for?" and gives Travis a dollar. Walter attempts to keep up the fantasy that they are not poor, for the sake of his son and his own pride. While Ruth is more pragmatic, Walter dreams of being able to provide for his family, symbolized in the small act of giving Travis the money.

Both Walter and Ruth work for white employers: Walter is a chauffeur, and Ruth is a housekeeper. Though exhausted from her job, Ruth does not share her husband's obsession with money and social standing; she would be satisfied with a peaceful home and an average income. The check they are waiting for is the insurance payment for Walter's father's death. Walter believes wealth will lead to independence and security, and he plans to open a liquor store with his friend Willy Harris. He is tired of his demeaning job and dreams of having the kind of life his wealthy boss possesses. Walter is one of the most vibrant and complex characters in the play. He is impulsive, irascible, desperate, and flawed, yet he is also a man seeking dignity, which he believes can be bought. Ruth places little faith in Walter's schemes to quickly fix the family's troubles. As Walter talks of his plans, she returns him to their daily reality, telling him to eat his eggs.

The next character to appear onstage is Walter's younger sister, Beneatha, "as slim and intense as her brother." Hansberry sets Beneatha apart from the others in describing her voice, "different from the rest of the family's insofar as education has permeated her sense of English." Beneatha, a college student, plans to go to medical school to become a doctor. Although Beneatha is not the protagonist, she is one of the most memorable characters. The critic Rachelle S. Gold describes her complexity:

> She is a budding feminist, educated, knowledgeable about her African heritage, skeptical about religion's role as a pacifying force, and sensitive to how class barriers restrict her from certain social relationships. . . . Complex and charismatic, her position in the play is murky. She is loveable and frustrating, unimportant, yet pivotal. She is absolutely one of the most memorable characters, vital to the character development, and yet she is irrelevant and expendable to the main conflict in the play. (17)

Act I, scene 1 captures the antagonistic dynamics between brother and sister that dominate their interactions throughout the play. They are both strong willed, stubborn, and prone to argument. Their first disagreement concerns the insurance check, a symbol of their hopes and dreams. In the first part of the play, money is the focal point of everyone's conversation.

At first, it seems that Beneatha, unlike her brother, expects nothing from the insurance check: "That money belongs to Mama, Walter, and it's for her to decide how she wants to use it." Yet the audience learns that a part of the insurance check will be set aside for Beneatha's education, about which Mama later asserts, "Ain't nothing going to touch that part of it. Nothing." Knowing that her tuition will absorb a portion of the payment, Walter lashes out at Beneatha: "Who the hell told you you had to be a doctor? If you so crazy 'bout messing round with sick people—then go be a nurse like other women—or just get married and be quiet." Walter's undermining of Beneatha's dreams reveals his chauvinism: "On one level Walter Lee is merely aspiring to full and acknowledged humanity; on another level he yearns to strut his 'manhood,' a predictable mix of *machismo* and fantasy" (Baraka 13). Because he gave his car fare to Travis, before Walter can leave for his job, he must ask Ruth for money, which adds to his building frustration and feelings of emasculation.

Beneatha does not let her brother's chauvinistic opinions about women stop her from achieving her dreams. A strong, intense woman, Beneatha is an early feminist, though the word *feminist* is never used. During the time period in which the play is set, the late 1950s, a female doctor would have been unusual, and an African-American female doctor would have been even more atypical. The social prejudices and obstacles that potentially awaited Beneatha would have been daunting. However, Beneatha is not discouraged, despite societal views toward blacks and women. Beneatha believes the world still offers her many possibilities. She is young and energetic, and, unlike Ruth and Walter, she does not work or worry as much about money.

The last major, and most pivotal, character to enter the room is Lena Younger (Mama), "a woman in her early sixties, full-bodied and strong. She is one of those women of a certain grace and beauty who wear it so unobtrusively that it takes a while to notice." Mama is highly religious; possesses a deep, abiding love for her family; and is the backbone of the family. She makes up Travis's bed on the couch, a simple task that hints at her maternal tenderness and strong love for her grandson.

In the same moment, in an overbearing and nosy manner, she questions (and doubts) Ruth about how she prepared Travis's breakfast. Mama, both caring and bossy, wants to put everyone's life in order and to maintain control.

Like the feeble, scraggly plant that she takes care of, giving it enough water and light for it to survive even under less than ideal conditions, Mama wants to help her family. However, she will not support Walter's plan to invest in a liquor store, which she views as immoral: "I don't want that on my ledger this late in life." Though Mama values the importance of education and of the future work of her daughter as a doctor, she does not believe they can become business owners: "We just plain working folks." In contrast to her earlier conversation with Walter, Ruth attempts to show support for Walter, believing that if Mama would give him some of the money, he may regain his confidence and happiness. Ruth recognizes that a part of Walter's spirit will die unless he can believe in the true possibility of change, and she hopes that restoring his confidence will also rekindle what has been lost between them: "I don't know what it is—but he needs something—something I can't give him anymore."

Once Ruth realizes she cannot convince Mama to invest in Walter's business plan, she tries to indulge Mama in fantasy, "Forget about the family and have yourself a ball for once in your life," playfully suggesting that Mama take a trip to Europe: "Shoot—these here rich white women do it all the time. They don't think nothing of packing up they suitcases and piling on one of them big steamships and—swoosh!—they gone, child." Mama responds, "Something always told me I wasn't no rich white woman." Mama, unlike her son, is a realist; she fully grasps society's harsh divisions of class and race, boundaries that she understands are nearly impossible for many to cross.

Mama believes the best way to use the money, in addition to supplementing Beneatha's education, is to buy a house, "a little old two-story somewhere, with a yard where Travis could play in the summertime." Ruth, who dreams of escaping their poor South Side neighborhood and living in a nice home, supports her in this decision. It has been a sustained dream of Mama's to live in a house. When she and her husband, the late Big Walter, first moved into their apartment many years ago, they planned on saving for a house; but over the years of hard work and struggle, the dream was constantly deferred: "But Lord, child you should know all the dreams I had 'bout buying that house and fixing it up and making me a little garden in the back. . . . And didn't none of it happen." The realities of racism, segregation, and economic struggle have kept the Youngers far from their dreams and squashed their opportunities. Mama recalls what Big Walter used to say: "Seem like God didn't see fit to give the black man nothing but dreams—but He did give us children to make them dreams seem worth while." The small, scraggly plant has served as a temporary stand-in for Mama's larger dream. Though Mama has always wanted a house with a garden, "This plant is close as I ever got to having one." Mama continues to believe in her dream, which helps her to persevere, but the dream is also tenuous, and often it is difficult for her to see beyond the present situation. Now, the death of her husband and her memories of him rekindle Mama's dream; ironically, it is through her husband's death that her dream has a chance to be realized.

When Beneatha returns from the bathroom, she mentions taking guitar lessons, and Mama teases her about her many pursuits: "Why you got to flit so from one thing to another, baby?" Beneatha is defensive about this "flitting," considering her artistic self-expression and need for self-realization as significant quests. Self-important about her intellectual and artistic pursuits, and immersed in her own dreams and fancies, Beneatha pays little attention to the rest of the family's worries. When Mama asks, "What is it you want to express?" Beneatha angrily bursts out, "Me!" which sends Mama and Ruth into bouts of laughter. Insulted, Beneatha tells them, "Don't worry—I don't expect you to understand." Beneatha often uses her education as a method of distancing herself from her family, as critic Rachelle S. Gold points out:

Beneatha uses two modes of knowledge to separate herself from her family, one where she merely broadcasts her beliefs, without asking anyone to subscribe to them, and one where she elevates her belief system over theirs, which highlights how Hansberry demonstrates the lack of "understanding" between the generations in the play. (7)

Beneatha is savvy and knowledgeable but also petulant, sassy, and argumentative, a character who embodies many contradictions. Gold provides a convincing analysis of Beneatha's dynamics with her family:

When she substitutes the values she learned in her internal home sphere with the cultural and ideological values that she learns in college, an external sphere, her family finds her threatening. Compassionate and yet judgmental, she is both peripheral and central to the play's action. Her role juxtaposes the old and the new, and as a mixture of these two perspectives, she is complicated because of her paradoxical nature. (3)

In terms of constructing her identity, Beneatha speaks out against assimilation, and, as she reveals in later scenes, feels strongly about connecting to African culture. Yet at the same time, she enjoys middle-class luxuries, including acting lessons and horseback riding, which Mama and Ruth, who have never had such opportunities, view as impractical. Beneatha desires to experience extracurricular activities of the middle and upper classes, which are often considered "white" pursuits, but also wants to live her life outside the dominant white culture. "She is, on the one hand, secure in the collegiate world of 'ideas' and elitism, above the mass; on the other, undeceived by the myths and symbols of class and status," attests Baraka. "Part militant, part dilettante, 'liberated' woman, little girl, she questions everything and dreams of service to humanity, an identity beyond self and family in the liberation struggles of her people" (14).

While Mama, as the oldest member of the family, is the backbone of the clan and its source of wisdom, Beneatha, as the youngest (other than Travis) symbolizes change and the spirit of the new. At the time the play was written, feminism had not fully emerged into the American landscape as it would in the 1960s; Beneatha, an early feminist, desires to pursue an independent career and is the least traditional of the women in the play. When she explains that she will not marry for wealth and that she may even decide not to marry, Mama and Ruth are shocked; in their experiences, a woman must follow society's expectations. Although Beneatha's political and religious views often separate her from her family, at the deepest level, Beneatha desires many of the same things—an improved life for her family and the opportunity for African Americans to better themselves through education, professional opportunity and advancement, and social and political action. However, her untraditional views are often a source of tension. When Beneatha tells her mother that she does not believe in God, Mama reacts by slapping her across the face and commanding her to say, "In my mother's house there is still a God."

This dramatic scene depicts Mama as the matriarch of the family; at this point, nobody questions or challenges (at least not without repercussions) her authority: "There are some ideas we ain't going to have in this house. Not long as I am at the head of this family." As the eldest, Mama represents traditional African Americans who found personal fulfillment, as well as the courage to take political and social action, in religious faith. In her chapter "*A Raisin in the Sun*: The Strong Black Woman as Acceptable Tyrant," the critic Trudier Harris examines how Mama represents the stereotypical matriarchal figure in African-American families. Her size, stature, and her name, Mama, reveal her to be a character of immense power and strength. Harris asserts that Mama's authority, "which begins with her name and her physical size and is very quickly bolstered by her Christianity," (24) also contributes to her self-righteous and tyrannical behavior. In this scene "it is the 'Mama' position that has given Mama Lena the 'right' to slap Beneatha, thereby making name, size, biology, and morality equal parts of the authority she wields" (27). She looms over her daughter, "and the daughter drops her eyes from her mother's face, and Mama is very tall before her." **Act I, scene 1** establishes Mama as the head of the family; she is the decision maker and the disciplinarian. She will retain control of the money and discipline her daughter for expressing ideas she does not agree with.

While Mama takes pride in her daughter's plan for medical school, she fears many of Beneatha's other ideas and admits to Ruth that her children frighten her:

> there's something come down between me and them that don't let us understand each other and I don't know what it is. One done almost lost his mind thinking 'bout money all the time and the other done commence to talk about things I can't seem to understand in no form or fashion. What is it that's changing, Ruth?

Through the characters, Hansberry examines the differences between the younger and older generations and how their varied experiences often create a gulf of separation between them. Critic Anne Cheney posits:

> the old world of Lena and the new world of Beneatha are separated by more than forty years of social and political change. The old world looks inward to the kitchen, the family, the home; the new world stares outward at college, medical school, Africa. Since the Younger family is searching for a center, a nucleus, the old and new world cannot orbit peacefully. (61)

Act I, scene 1 introduces the major characters, sets up the plot, and establishes many of the play's thematic elements. At the end of the scene, Ruth faints, adding another layer of tension to the plot.

3.

Act I, scene 2 opens the next morning, a Saturday, when "house cleaning is in progress." This scene presents the Younger pride that Mama tries to instill in her children; although they are poor and do not own much, the apartment will sparkle.

This means so much to Mama that when Asagai telephones, Beneatha is reluctant to invite him over because she knows that her mother does not want company to see the apartment in disarray. Although the play takes place entirely within the Youngers' apartment, external influences heighten the drama. In this scene, there are two phone calls—one for Beneatha and one for Walter. Walter's caller is Willy, the man behind the idea to invest in a liquor store. Walter assures him, "I told you the mailman doesn't get here till ten-thirty," reminding the audience that today is the day the check will arrive.

After Walter leaves, Ruth enters and says what Mama has guessed is true, that she is pregnant. Mama at first tries to rally Ruth, happily exclaiming, "Lord have mercy, I sure hope it's a little old girl. Travis ought to have a sister." In a moment that connects the younger generations, Ruth and Beneatha "give her a hopeless look for this grandmotherly enthusiasm," both knowing that another child will add more strain to the delicate financial situation. Mama asks Ruth what the doctor said, and Ruth, listless and sad, replies, "she says everything is going to be fine" and Mama is "immediately suspicious" by the slip of the pronoun: "What doctor you went to?"

Meanwhile, there is commotion outside the window: Travis is with the neighborhood kids, chasing a rat. Beneatha yells at him to get upstairs, and he runs in the apartment, breathlessly describing how the shopkeeper chased and then killed the rat. The violence of the story causes Ruth to clamp her hand over his mouth, and Mama says, "You hush up now . . . talking all that terrible stuff" and sends Travis back outside. Ruth, clenching her fist, "is fighting hard to suppress a scream that seems to be rising in her" until she collapses "into a fit of heavy sobbing." In the original production, the rat chase was cut out and was later reinserted; it is a vivid depiction of the daily terrors that confronted the children of the poor, a scene symbolic of the conditions they live in, what Beneatha refers to as "acute ghetto-itis." The rat scene also emphasizes the family's impending doom and the feeling of entrapment that marks their existence.

In **act I, scene 2,** a new character shows up—Beneatha's college friend, Asagai, a Nigerian. He has just returned to Chicago, after spending the summer studying in Canada. Asagai, racially proud and handsome, is an intellectual and political activist. Through his character, Hansberry introduces her audience to African history and society and examines the complicated dynamics between African Americans and Africans. Before Asagai arrives, Beneatha warns her mother not to embarrass her by asking ignorant questions about Africa, depicting the generational difference and intellectual gap that exists between Mama and Beneatha. She rightly assumes that her mother's ideas of Africa are limited to images of Tarzan and from what she has learned in church about Christians saving them from "heathenism." As Beneatha explains that the only saving the Africans need is political and civil freedom from French and British colonialism, "Hansberry deliberately sets out to subvert common erroneous beliefs about Africa, and uses Beneatha as her mouthpiece" (Effiong 40). In 1959, the majority of Americans, white and black, knew little about Africa, aside from what they saw in mainstream films or broadcasts from the various colonial powers. When Mama meets Asagai, she is polite and gracious and dutifully recites what Beneatha told her about Nigeria and the politics of colonialism.

Throughout the play, the audience gains insights into African history, politics, and philosophy, as is initially depicted in this scene. Asagai gives Beneatha African records and "the colorful robes of a Nigerian woman," and then he playfully teases Beneatha for her "mutilated hair." Beneatha is genuinely disturbed, especially when he implies that, in looking "for her identity," she does not truly grasp her African roots. "Assimilationism is so popular in your country," he teases, referring to the straightening of her hair, which she does, in his view, in order to meet a Hollywood-created or European standard of beauty. Beneatha wheels around, furious, "I am not an assimilationist!"

Beneatha is caught between worlds. She wants the opportunities that then existed predominately in upper-class, white society, but she also does not want to assimilate to the dominant white culture of the 1950s. Like many African-American intellectuals and writers, she faces a dilemma. She wants to break free of the white American ideal yet also wants the traditional trappings and benefits of an educated existence. Beneatha is a character ahead of her time, in terms of both her feminism and her desire to seek out her African roots, a desire that predates and anticipates the New African movement of the 1960s, in which African Americans stopped attempting to assimilate and looked to African history and culture, in order to claim and establish their identity.

Though politically progressive, Asagai displays some of the same chauvinistic views as his male counterparts. When he tells Beneatha that this "feeling between a man and woman" should be enough, she argues, "I know—because that's what it says in all the novels that men write. But it isn't. Go ahead and laugh—but I'm not interested in being someone's little episode in America." Storybook love is not enough for Beneatha. As a strong and independent woman, she initially rejects Asagai. Yet, she is also charmed, especially when he calls her by the African name, Alaiyo, which means "one for whom bread—food—is not enough."

After Asagai leaves, Beneatha studies herself in the mirror, holding the Nigerian dress up and setting the headdress on her head. She "then notices her hair again and clutches at it and then replaces the headdress and frowns at herself." When Travis asks what is wrong, she announces that she is going to "become a queen of the Nile!" and "exits in a breathless blaze of glory."

Meanwhile, the anticipation of the insurance check is growing. When the doorbell rings at 10:30, it "sounds suddenly and sharply and all three are stunned—serious and silent—mid-speech. In spite of all the other conversations and distraction of the morning, this is what they have been waiting for, even Travis who looks helplessly from his mother to his grandmother." Ruth is the first one to jump to life, instructing Travis to retrieve the mail. The excitement is contagious, with Mama holding her hand to her breast in disbelief: "You mean it done really come?" When Travis returns he "holds the envelope high above his head, like a little dancer, his face is radiant and he is breathless. He moves to his grandmother with sudden slow ceremony and puts the envelope into her hands." Travis and Ruth encourage Mama to open the envelope, but she sits staring at it, trying to calm herself, in disbelief: "Now don't act silly. . . . We ain't never been no people to act silly 'bout no money—" Finally, she opens it and stares in awe at the check, asking Travis if that is indeed the right number of zeros, and he confirms the amount, "ten thousand dollars." The scene captures Mama's bittersweet emotions; she is thrilled about what this check will do for the family yet feels grief and sadness that her husband had to die in order for them to realize their dreams. With her face a "mask of unhappiness," she laments, "Ten thousand dollars. . . . Ten thousand dollars they give you."

When Walter walks in, Mama, suspecting that Ruth is planning an abortion, instructs him to talk to his wife, but Walter only wants to talk about the check. Ruth, disgusted, responds, "Oh, let him go on out and drink himself to death! He makes me sick to my stomach!" and rushes into the bedroom. At this point, it is impossible for her to interrupt her husband's incessant speech. Mama, the voice of authority, treats Walter like a child and tells him for the last time, "And there ain't going to be no investing in no liquor stores." Walter reacts with anger and frustration, feeling that nobody listens to him or respects him. When Mama precludes his dream of opening the liquor store, he sees everything he associated with the investment crumbling before him: money, social status, and freedom. "Do you know what this money means to me? Do you know what this money can do for us?" Walter is ashamed of his poverty, his job, and his lack of upward mobility. "Sometimes it's like I can see the future stretched in front of me—just plain as day. The future, Mama. Hanging over there at the edge of my day. Just waiting for me—a big, looming blank space—full of nothing. Just waiting for me. But it don't have to be." Walter's deferred dreams have begun to crush him; he clings to them, internally, until they consume him.

Mama wants her son to follow his dreams, but she is disturbed by the way he considers money to be synonymous with life. Walter's dreams have become consumed and tainted by materialism. Mama comments, sadly, that once "freedom used to be life—now it's money." She sees Walter as "something new." Mama is part of the generation that "was worried about not being lynched and getting to the North if we could and how to say alive and still have a pinch of dignity too . . ." Members of Mama's generation worked hard so their children could have a better life, one without segregation, but Walter and his generation take freedom for granted.

Acting as the head of the family, Mama must convey to Walter the news of both Ruth's pregnancy and her impending abortion. Walter does not believe her, but then Ruth enters, finding her voice: "Yes I would too, Walter." She admits that she has put down a five-dollar payment to have the abortion, a strong statement coming from a woman who would not give her son fifty cents for school. Critic Trudier Harris describes Ruth as "basically mousy, quiescent. She can never claim a space as the primary woman in this household and is thereby pushed into a peripheral, ghostlike position" (28). Ruth's name is an allusion to the faithful biblical wife and daughter-in-law, and she is presented as the calmest in temperament, a woman who bridges the generations and often acquiesces to others in the name of harmony. Yet she also displays moments of quiet strength and determination. The three female characters each represent different generations: "Beneatha, Ruth, and Lena reflect the different roles of women in society—the old versus the new woman" (Cheney 61). Ruth falls between Beneatha and Mama, caught between tradition and the new ideas gaining societal credence. She values the traditional roles as wife and mother; yet she still considers having an abortion. In 1959, abortion was illegal; Hansberry is making a bold feminist statement with this addition to the plot. This was one of the first American plays to address abortion, which Ruth sees as the only way to keep the family together. It is also a scene that reveals Ruth's independence, expressing her right to choose and to assert control, yet it also depicts the desperation of a working-class woman who cannot afford to have another child.

Mama greatly opposes Ruth getting an abortion. Mama's religious beliefs and conservative views will not allow her to consider this as a possibility. The memory of Claude, the baby she lost, fuels her opposition. She challenges Walter, "I'm waiting to hear how you be your father's son. Be the man he was." Mama recalled earlier in the play how devastated Big Walter was by the loss of Claude, and now she wants to see her son respond similarly. She fears that Walter has given up all hope for himself and his progeny.

The concept of "being a man" and the construction of masculinity is another prominent theme in the play. Big Walter looms in the background of the play, serving as a moral force. He is presented as a flawed but good man who believed in his children and the possibilities of dreams. Mama describes him in **scene 1** as a "hard-headed man kind of wild with women—plenty wrong with him." Mama's marriage was not easy, but she never considered that it could be any other way. Mama equates masculinity with a husband/father taking charge; yet, at the same time, she has taken on many of these responsibilities herself and clearly feels comfortable in her husband's role. She is the center of her family's life and controls many of the interactions of the other family members. She also makes the economic decisions, as depicted literally in this scene in which she holds the insurance check in her hand. Thus, Mama does not give her son the option to follow in his father's footsteps, and Walter, who has been so consumed by materialistic dreams, is shocked into silence. He says nothing to Ruth in response to the news about the abortion, shaming Mama, who asserts: "You . . . you are a disgrace to your father's memory." Walter represents a broken masculinity, specifically pertaining to African-American men of the 1950s who were shut out of the American Dream by racism and economic oppression. Because of this exclusion, Walter's dreams of success and money become tied to his perceptions of himself and his manhood.

4.

Act II, scene 1 opens later that day, with Ruth at the ironing board. When Beneatha enters wearing the brightly colored Nigerian robes and headdress that Asagai gave her, "Ruth's mouth falls and she puts down the iron in fascination," a scene that contrasts Ruth's domestic lifestyle and her identity as a wife and mother with Beneatha's more worldly, international persona. Dancing to one of the African records that Asagai gave her, Beneatha looks "enraptured, her eyes far away— 'back to the past.'" She performs what she believes to be a Nigerian folk dance, shouting, "OCOMOGOSIAY!", and gives Ruth and the audience a lesson in its significance. Though Beneatha's intentions are sincere, Hansberry also describes her as "coquettishly fanning herself . . . mistakenly more like Butterfly than any Nigerian." Thus, Beneatha is more like the opera character Madame Butterfly instead of African royalty. This scene stresses Beneatha's complex relationship to Africa— her naiveté about African culture and her deep yearning to feel connected to what she believes are her roots.

When Walter, drunk, enters the apartment, he joins his sister, yelling, "FLAMING SPEAR!" He is being sarcastic, but Beneatha fails to interpret this, and she continues the performance with Walter. Their imitation of a Yoruba "dance of welcome" is itself a mockery but is also "magical and therapeutic, for [Beneatha] draws Walter into it and reaches out briefly to a brother who she despises" (Effiong 38). While Ruth looks on, the chanting and dancing seem to transform Walter, and he suddenly pulls his shirt open, jumps on the table, and pretends to hold a spear, yelling, "THE LION IS WAKING," referring to the African countries that were beginning to demand their independence from colonial rule during this period. The juxtaposition of the Youngers' cramped apartment with the imagined African village dramatizes the complexity of Africa and African-American relations.

This scene introduced early audiences to something they had never seen performed onstage before. On one hand, the sibling's imitation of an African tribal dance is problematic because it is stereotypical: "While Africa offers a vital historical and cultural frame of reference, it remains a distant land largely unknown and often illusory. Walter's drunken state during the sub drama only reinforces this dilemma" (Effiong 39). On the other hand, the African ceremonial dance also invokes racial pride and affinity between brother and sister. On the surface, Walter is depicted as comical, but as the scene continues, Walter reveals himself to be a sympathetic and tragic character. He attempts to recapture his lost African past, with "the inner Walter speaking: the Southside chauffeur has assumed an unexpected majesty" and becomes eloquent, experiencing racial pride and a renewed confidence in his manhood: "OH, DO YOU HEAR, MY BLACK BROTHERS! . . . Telling us to prepare for the GREATNESS OF THE TIME!" Critic Margaret B. Wilkerson characterizes Walter as signaling "the wave of the future. He is restless, hungry, angry—a victim of his circumstance but at the same time the descendant of his proud forebears, struggling to transcend his victimhood" (10). When Beneatha's date, George Murchison, enters, Walter greets him, "Black Brother," and George responds, "Black Brother, Hell!," immediately exstinguishing the powerful mood while simultaneously ending any possibility for racial brotherhood.

George Murchison is handsome, educated, and wealthy. He is the prototype of the black bourgeoisie, the opposite of Asagai. From the beginning, Beneatha has displayed a savvy approach to her relationship with George. While her family has hopes he will marry her, improving their own economic standing as a result, she understands that George is unlikely to marry her because she is from a different class. In the opening act, she describes George's family as "honest-to-God real-live rich colored people, and the only people in the world who are more snobbish than rich white people are rich colored people." George's family believes they can achieve respect through their economic status and a certain degree of assimilation to the dominant white culture. With George, Hansberry is able to closely examine class divisions in the African-American community and to further examine the role of Africa in African-American ideas about identity. When Beneatha lifts off the headdress to reveal the hairstyle that Asagai had encouraged her to get, "close-cropped and unstraightened," both George and Ruth are shocked, with Ruth exclaiming, "You expect this boy to go out with you with your head all nappy like that." This scene was most likely the first display of a Nigerian costume and natural hairstyle performed on the American stage. The scene validates the natural hairstyle (unstraightened hair on black women), a new concept in 1959, even considered somewhat radical when the play opened. The symbolism of the natural hair represents blackness and expresses Beneatha's attempted connection to Africa: "Her robe and natural 'afro' hair presage the new wave of fashion and hairstyles that were embraced by Black Americans in the 1960s" (Effiong 38).

Beneatha's afro incites a fierce argument between Beneatha and George about the importance of African heritage, which represents a larger battle about assimilation within the African-American community. George is smug and snobbish and scorns any connection to Africa: "Let's face it, baby, your heritage is nothing but a bunch of raggedy-assed spirituals and some grass huts!" While George belittles Beneatha's ideas of history and the heritage of black people, Hansberry astutely depicts the many layers of African versus America-based black identities, while continuing to educate her audience about Africa. Even George, who has learned about Africa in college, provides significant references, including his mention of the Songhay civilization, a powerful empire and western African kingdom during C.E. 850–1500. This particular reference reveals Hansberry's concern with the demise of such great civilizations and her regret that there was a lack of general knowledge of these ancient African kingdoms.

Beneatha accuses George of being "ashamed of his heritage" and explains that she will wear her hair this way, proudly, "Because I hate assimilationist Negroes!" As his common name suggests, George seeks assimilation, whereas Asagai, with his Nigerian name, stands for the New Africanist culture. By aligning herself with Asagai, Beneatha forges a closer connection to her African heritage. Before they leave for their date, George will change his mind when he sees Beneatha dressed in a cocktail dress, deciding that the hair is stylish: "I like it. It's sharp. I mean it really is." To him, when she is wearing a Western dress, the hair looks stylish and cutting edge, but when she is dressed in the African robes, the hair makes her look too "African."

While Beneatha changes her clothes, Walter tries to talk "business" with George, a crucial scene that symbolizes the significant division between poor African Americans and those of the middle and upper classes. Walter tries to use George to gain access to the young man's father, expressing admiration for him and depicting himself as a similar kind of businessman: "Man, I got me some ideas," he says. But George, bored, is dismissive of Walter's "big" business plans. George's pedantic personality insults Walter, who retorts "You colored college boys with your fraternity pins and white shoes. . . . I see you all the time—with the books tucked under your arms. . . . Filling up your heads—but they teaching you how to be a man?" Jealous of George's wealth, Walter tries to belittle him by equating college with weakness. By mocking George's white shoes, he reveals his own insecurity and dependence on machismo. Walter feels that manhood is wrapped up in a man's ability to make money. But Hansberry, in questioning the construction of masculinity, also demonstrates how Walter has been locked out of the opportunities that George has been given. Critic Lloyd W. Brown suggests that George's "bourgeois materialism illustrates the American propensity to confuse material achievement with the total promise of the American dream" but argues that Walter has similar ambitions, that "the deprived and the disadvantaged are like the affluent bourgeoisie in that they, too, view materialistic achievements as self-justifying, even self-redeeming, goals" (242).

This scene captures Walter's pent-up rage, portraying him as a man "wacked up with bitterness," and "a volcano" about to become destructive. George snidely refers to Walter as "Prometheus," a reference that Walter does not understand but takes as an insult. Prometheus was a Greek god punished for bringing fire to mortals; he was chained to Mount Caucasus, where his liver was torn out every day by an eagle, then grew back each night. His suffering lasted for thousands of years, until Hercules killed the eagle and freed Prometheus. The name is symbolic of Walter's suffering and displays the gulf between Walter and George. Walter is "an outsider on two counts: he is both Black and poor. Hence, Walter's unabashed obsession with the insurance money as a key to instant affluence fits the materialistic priorities of the outsider's dream" (Brown 243). Walter has been shut out of the American Dream, and his desire to attain this dream all the more only deepens his sense of frustration and disappointment.

After Beneatha and George leave for their date, Ruth and Walter, alone in the apartment, begin to bicker, until Ruth, defeated, implores Walter, "Honey, why can't you stop fighting me?" Ruth wants to save her marriage but feels that it is too late: "I don't know where we lost it . . . but we have." For the first time in the play, Walter acknowledges the distance between them, as they speak candidly about their loss of affection and hope. Ruth attempts to nurture her husband, asking him if he wants her to heat up milk. Walter feels emasculated and infantilized: "Why are you always trying to give me something to eat?" But Ruth does not know how to make him happy: "What else can I give you, Walter Lee Younger?"

This scene is one of the more intimate scenes between Ruth and Walter, when Walter admits, "It's been rough, ain't it, baby? . . . How we gets to the place where we scared to talk softness to each other." Ruth senses a moment of vulnerability in Walter, a chance perhaps to rekindle their love and instill in him the confidence he needs. "Honey . . . life don't have to be like this. . . . You remember how we used to talk when Travis was born. . . . Well, it's all starting to slip away from us." Walter and Ruth reminisce about the early days of their relationship, contrasting the dreams of that former time to the more dire conditions that mark their present reality, in which "something done come down between us." There is still love left in their marriage, but they have been oppressed by their difficult situation.

Just as they are beginning to reconcile, Mama unexpectedly returns. She has been out all day, trying to make things better for a family that she fears is falling apart: "We couldn't of gone on like we was today. We was going backwards 'stead of forwards." Mama then reveals that she has made a down payment on a house, a place where "there's a yard with a little batch of dirt where I could maybe get to grow me a few flowers." Displaying the full sway of her authority, Mama bought the house without consulting anyone else. At first, Ruth is ecstatic and grateful, but her excitement temporarily diminishes when Mama tells them that the house is in Clybourne Park, a white neighborhood. Ruth responds: "Clybourne Park? Mama, there ain't no colored people living in Clybourne Park."

Mama's main concern is to buy a nice home for her family, and "them houses they put up for colored in them areas way out all seem to cost twice as much as other houses." She is not moving to Clybourne Park because she necessarily wants to integrate a white neighborhood; rather, she wants the greatest value for her money. Mama believes that in order for the family to be happy, they need their own space; it is the quintessential post–World War II American belief, that ownership and possessions could provide happiness. Yet Mama is also a radical in attempting to attain this dream, as African Americans, especially the poor, were barred from or left out of the dream of upward mobility. Critic Lloyd W. Brown explains:

> Hence the basic contextual irony of the title, and of the themes which flow from it, is based on an acceptance of the dream ideal—spiritual and material fulfillment in America—and, simultaneously, on a realistic recognition of those (like Walter Younger) whose dreams, or hopes, have dried up. The point is not that Lorraine Hansberry rejects integration or the economic and moral promise of the American dream, but that she remains loyal to this dream ideal while looking, realistically, at its corruption in the United States. (240)

Their dreams have been deferred because they must struggle for economic survival. Thus, Hansberry performs a radical act in presenting an African-American family staking a claim on a life commonly associated with middle-class white Americans.

Though she is frightened, Ruth cannot contain her happiness. She emerges from her shell in a flurry of passion, pounding the walls of the apartment, and exclaiming, "Then I say it loud and good, HALLELUJAH! AND GOOD-BYE MISERY.... I DON'T NEVER WANT TO SEE YOUR UGLY FACE AGAIN!" She is overcome, laughing and joyous, and asks Mama, "Is there—is there a whole lot of sunlight?" The new house represents a way out of the darkness, and Mama replies: "Yes, child, there's a whole lot of sunlight." Only Walter is unhappy, bitterly accusing his mother of "butcher[ing] up a dream of mine." His angry, desperate outburst makes Mama feel guilty, and she worries about her son.

5.

Act II, scene 2 opens a few weeks later, on a Friday night. Packing crates fill the apartment, in preparation for the move. George and Beneatha come in from an evening out and quickly get into an argument, in which George's know-it-all attitude is on full display. He tells Beneatha that he views college only as a way to get ahead: "You read books—to learn facts—to get grades—to pass the course—to get a degree. That's all—it has nothing to do with thoughts." This scene makes George and Beneatha's incompatibility clear, and their strong philosophical differences all the more apparent. George views college as an economic steppingstone, whereas for Beneatha, college is a way to expand her mind, to express herself, and to grow. Beneatha understands that, unlike her and Asagai, George does not value learning and that he also does not respect her as a woman. He tells her that what he wants from a woman is not intellectual conversation: "I don't go out with you to discuss the nature of 'quiet desperation' or to hear all about your thoughts." George tells her that men do not like opinionated, liberated women. Throughout the play, Beneatha must reject a chorus of sexist male voices—from Asagai, Walter, and George. As a strong black woman, Beneatha is an outsider on several levels; within the African-American community exists the even more marginalized group of women, facing and fighting prejudice expressed along both racial and gender lines.

Beneatha finally cuts her bourgeois ties by telling George to leave. Although Beneatha's views are radically different from George's, she also does not fit neatly into her own family's working-class world. Therefore she is surprised when her mother supports her: "Well—I guess you better not waste your time with no fools." Beneatha thanks her for understanding. Mama's support indicates a softening of the tensions that have hurt their relationship. Furthermore, although George's status and wealth at first impressed Mama, she eventually comes to share Beneatha's point of view. Mama's strong opinions and support of her daughter's values are further demonstrated in the scene with the nosy Mrs. Johnson.

Mrs. Johnson enters sharing the latest news headlines, "You mean you ain't read 'bout them colored people that was bombed out their place out there," referring to the violence and hatred an African-American family faced when they moved to a white neighborhood. Her intent is to belittle the importance of the Youngers leaving the ghetto. She speaks about it in an uncivil manner, predicting the Youngers will be driven out of the white neighborhood. In addition to characterizing Mrs. Johnson as insensitive, the reference to the bomb also provides the audience with an example of the real danger the Youngers face in moving. This scene clearly situates the Youngers in 1959 Chicago, depicting the racist political and social atmosphere that predominated at the time.

Mrs. Johnson provides comic relief and, more significantly, serves as a foil to Mama. In the original production, this scene was cut from the play, and it is still often omitted from productions. However, it is a significant representation of clashing ideologies; Mrs. Johnson clarifies the Youngers' perspective by representing its opposite. She looks down on the Youngers for trying to partake in a dream she believes does not belong to them: "It's just—you know how some of our young people gets when they get a little education." Instead, she thinks they should value hard work, like Walter's "good job," which causes Mama to counter, "There's plenty wrong with it." In this scene, the audience gets a better understanding of Mama's political leanings and also of her empathy toward her son: "My husband always said being any kind of a servant wasn't a fit thing for a man to have to be. . . . And my boy is just like him—he wasn't meant to wait on nobody." Perhaps, too, Mama has been mulling over and empathizing with Walter's desperate dreams to escape his present life.

Mrs. Johnson exclaims, "You sure one proud-acting bunch of colored folks" and follows this by quoting a line by Booker T. Washington: "Education has spoiled many a good plow hand." Mama quickly replies, "Well, it sounds just like him. The fool." In this exchange, Hansberry is examining the contrasting philosophies of African-American leaders Booker T. Washington (1856–1915) and W.E.B. Du Bois (1868–1963). Washington, an influential leader immediately following Reconstruction, believed that blacks should be educated by trade skills and that artistic endeavors and intellectual pursuits were not in the best interest of people trying to emerge from a long period of slavery. A hero to many in the black community, Washington preached assimilation to mainstream America as the primary goal of African Americans. He attained great stature in the first half of the twentieth century, but public opinion turned against him by the late 1950s. Black writers, intellectuals, and artists tended to side with Du Bois, who believed in the importance of artistic endeavors. The comical character of Mrs. Johnson acts as the defender of Washington, while Hansberry voices her own support for Du Bois through Mama, who seems to be developing more of an understanding of her children's modern ideas. Anne Cheney astutely argues that "the old world of Lena and the new world of Beneatha cannot remain static. As both worlds react and collide with the other, they are sure to emerge as slightly different substances. Little is lost in these transformations. Much is gained in the new structure of strength, humanity, wisdom" (65).

Mama fully grasps the depth of her son's despair when she finds out that Walter, depressed, has not gone to work for three days. Instead, he has taken long drives to look at the farms and steel mills that, to Walter, represent true success and manhood.

All are out of reach for him, and, in his despair, he spends his nights drinking and listening to jazz and the blues. Mama can no longer stand to see him in such a state, and she makes a significant decision: to relinquish her power and the money to her son. She tells him there is nothing so precious to her if "it's going to destroy my boy." Mama made a down payment for $3,500 on the new house, which left $6,500, which she gives to Walter. She tells him to put $3,000 in the bank for medical school for Beneatha and the rest into a checking account that he will oversee: "I'm telling you to be the head of this family from now on like you supposed to be." Walter is filled with renewed hope and confidence, and "in a decisive gesture, he gets up, and in mingled joy and desperation, picks up the money."

In a touching and tension-building scene, Walter encourages his son, Travis, to envision a future filled with opportunities, a future in which he will not have to settle to work as "a bus driver." When Walter reveals that he's "gonna make a transaction . . . a business transaction that's going to change our lives," a new conflict or challenge potentially emerges. From Walter's fantastical talk, the audience infers that he will not invest wisely. This underlying tension builds until the climax in **act II, scene 3**. As Walter describes the future, he mentions coming home from the office, and Travis reminds him, "You don't work in no office, Daddy." Even Travis, a ten-year-old, discerns fantasy from reality. But Walter cannot stop, and, as he talks, the dream grows more elaborate and impossibly out of reach. Walter believes that the money will give him the kind of life that Mr. Arnold, his wealthy white employer, leads, that he will have an expensive car, a gardener named Jefferson, and a work day characterized by "conferences and secretaries." Walter, as Cheney points out, has been "duped by the American dream" (68). He still wants to be part of the culture that excludes him and believes wealth will be the solution to his family's problems:

> Not only does Walter Lee feel powerless in this own family before Mama gives him control of the legacy, but he feels impotent within the black community. His

admiration for the upwardly mobile black, in fact, leads to a serious flaw in his judgment: he considers Willy Harris a successful businessman when he is really an untrustworthy hustler. (Cheney 59)

Walter is unrealistic but not selfish. He hopes Travis will have a better life than he has had so far, and he wants to offer Travis a strong image and model of a father; Walter does not want wealth only for the sake of being rich but sees increased prosperity as a means to better housing, education, social position, and human dignity.

6.

Act I, scene 3 opens one week later, on moving day, a Saturday. Ruth and Beneatha, in good spirits, are packing. Ruth is musing about the house and says the first thing she wants to do is "run me a tub of water up to here. . . . And I'm going to get in it—and I am going to sit . . . and sit . . . and sit in that hot water." The dynamics between Ruth and Walter have changed since Mama relinquished control of the check; they are happy again and hopeful. Ruth tells Beneatha they went on a date to the movies, their first outing in a long time, and "held hands." As if to confirm the improved marital relations, a joyful Walter enters. He turns on the record player and dances with Ruth to a slow song; he is playful, happy, even pleasant with Beneatha. A resurgence of faith has gripped the members of the Younger household. The marriage that was troubled in the beginning of the play is now transformed and reborn.

Yet an element of tension threatens to destabilize the joyful mood when the doorbell rings and a white man, "a representative of the Clybourne Park Improvement Association," announces that he is there to see Lena Younger. Walter, acting as "head of the household," tells him that he now takes care of his mother's business matters, and he invites him in. The sole white character in the play, Karl Lindner is an ineffectual presence, "gentle," and "somewhat labored in his manner." Lindner explains that problems only arise when different kinds of people do not sit down and talk to one another, and Walter, unsure of the man's purpose, agrees. Lindner does not address race directly but uses ambiguous, euphemistic language, and Walter and Ruth are unsure of his intent. Beneatha, however, distrusts him immediately, symbolizing her quick and astute judgment.

Walter and Ruth do not understand until Lindner explains that he was selected to speak with them to discuss how "our Negro families are happier when they live in their own communities." Lindner wants to pay the Youngers not to make the move to the new neighborhood. He says he will make them "a very generous offer" for them to stay in their present home. In this scene, the audience witnesses Walter's pride for his race and his family, when he angrily refuses the offer and tells Linder to get out. The critic Helene Kennsyer points out the complexity of Hansberry's portrayal of the Youngers achieving the American Dream:

> Hansberry has succeeded in persuading the audience to the legitimacy of the Youngers' aspirations, but she has simultaneously shown the extreme difficulty, if not impossibility, for this family of fulfilling their dreams of change, stability, and comfort. Hansberry directly undercuts the central middle-class American notion of "equality of opportunity" by presenting the white man, Mr. Lindner, who finally believes that opportunities for blacks should not be identical with those for whites. (143)

After Lindner leaves, Mama enters, and her children tell her about "the Welcoming Committee." In disgust, Mama throws Lindner's business card on the floor, fully understanding the many faces of racism. The Youngers are not intimidated but are warned of the possibility of impending conflict. Referring to their future white neighbors, Beneatha says, "What they think we going to do—eat 'em?" Ruth quips, "No, honey, marry 'em." This exchange is a commentary on the racism of the North, the fears of integration and miscegenation. But the Youngers will not allow racism to derail their plan for a better life. Despite the negativity that Lindner brought into the house, the Youngers try to regain their happiness and confidence. Mama fusses with her plant, and when Beneatha asks why she wants to take that "raggedly-looking old thing" to the new house, Mama responds, "It expresses ME!" As Rachelle S. Gold points out, "In this way, Mama is able to deflect the power of Beneatha's insult by using the word 'expresses,' which is the same word Beneatha uses when claiming what her hobbies do for her" (9). The plant symbolizes Mama's fortitude in holding onto her dream.

Soon Mama will have not only a plant but a plot of land, a garden. The plant depicts Mama's love of the land: "Her nurturance of the plant reflects the caring associated with both mothers and agrarians" (Cheney 62). The family gathers around Mama to surprise her with a set of gardening tools, and Travis gives her a "very elaborate, wide gardening hat," which provides a moment of comic relief. The hat, in his eyes, is a symbol of her new status as a more affluent woman. Ironically, the hat serves to make Mama look more like a field hand than a wealthy woman, "like you ready to go out and chop you some cotton sure enough!" The family is in high spirits, hopeful, with Walter singing, "I got wings, You got wings! All God's children got wings!"

The doorbell rings again. This time, standing there is "a very slight little man in a not too prosperous business suit and with haunted frightened eyes." Walter introduces him as Bobo, one of Walter's business partners. Walter notes that Willy is not with him but does not seem disturbed by Willy's absence or Bobo's worried look. Ruth, however, senses something is wrong, and she "stands stiffly and quietly in back of them, as though somehow she senses death, her eyes fixed on her husband." The tension builds as Bobo tries to tell Walter about Willy. Near tears, he finally says, "Man—Willy *didn't never show up*," revealing that Willy ran off with the money. At first, Walter tries to find excuses, but Bobo exclaims, "What's the matter with you, Walter! When a cat take off with our money he don't leave you no road maps!" Though Willy never makes an appearance onstage, he remains a faceless symbol of Walter's negligence—the focus is not on the act of theft but on the reactions of the family to adversity.

Walter, wild, turns in circles, even begins to "crumple down on the floor as Ruth just covers her face in horror." This is Walter's breaking point, when he finally realizes his grievous mistake, exploding with feelings of helplessness, anger, and grief: "THAT MONEY IS MADE OUT OF MY FATHER'S FLESH." When Mama asks Walter if all of the money is gone, he admits that he never went to the bank. He gave Willy all of it, including Beneatha's medical school money. In the face of the loss, Mama's idealism about her family falters. Stunned, she stares at her son, then starts to beat him in the face. She wants Walter to realize his mistakes, explaining how she witnessed her husband "working and working and working like somebody's old horse . . . killing himself . . . and you—you give it all away in a day." But Mama has not lost her faith; she appeals to God in the end, as weakness overcomes her, and she prays for strength.

7.

Act III opens an hour later, with the apartment now returning to the way it looked at the beginning of the play: "At curtain, there is a sullen light of gloom in the living room, gray light not unlike that which began the first scene of Act One." Walter is in his room, alone, stretched out in the bed, stricken: "He does not smoke, he does not cry out, he merely lies there, looking up at the ceiling, much as if he were alone in the world."

Meanwhile, Asagai shows up "smiling broadly, striding into the room with energy and happy expectation and conversation." He does not know anything about the family's financial loss, until he is greeted by a changed Beneatha who tells him that the money to finance her medical training is gone. In this scene, the audience learns what compelled Beneatha to want to become a doctor. Unlike her many "flitting" hobbies—guitar lessons and horseback riding, for example—her dream to become a doctor is unselfish and deeply rooted, inspired by a childhood friend's accident. Beneatha wants to help the sick and needy, to help her fellow human beings become better: "I wanted to cure."

Beneatha tells Asagai that her dreams have been destroyed, expecting sympathy from him, but instead he criticizes her for her materialistic outlook. Asagai questions the Western definition of success and the kind of happiness that is dependent on the death of a loved one: "Then isn't there something wrong in a house—in a world—where all dreams, good or bad, must depend on the death of a man?" Asagai is the play's steadfast idealist, whereas Beneatha falters, giving up hope: "Don't you see there isn't any real progress, Asagai, there is only one large circle that we march in, around and around, each of us with our own little picture in front of us—our own little mirage which we think is the future." Now, her own dreams disintegrated, Beneatha broods about basic human misery and no longer sees a reason to fight against it. "Because it doesn't seem deep enough, close enough to what ails mankind! It was a child's way of seeing things—or an idealist's."

Asagai defends the idealist stance: "Children see things very well sometimes—and idealists even better." Their conversation expands into a discussion of Africa, and Asagai talks of his dream to return to his country, in order to bring about positive changes. Asagai symbolizes the struggle for liberation, telling Beneatha that one mistake does not stop a movement. At first, Beneatha responds cynically: "You with all your talk and dreams about Africa! You still think you can patch up the world. Cure the Great Sore of Colonialism." Asagai's belief that the colonial powers must fall predicts the unrest to occur in those countries following the 1950s; at the same time, Beneatha's retort about the corruption of many African leaders also rings true. Thus, Africa in the play becomes a symbol of proud heritage, with a hopeful but troublesome future, as critic Philip Uko Effiong explains:

> Irrespective of how laudable some of the images of Africa are in *A Raisin*, Hansberry does not romanticize the yearning for a culturally rich, spiritual homeland. Africa also surfaces as a background afflicted by political weaknesses that have existed for generations. . . . [T]here are also skeptical hints at possible flaws within

independent Africa. When Asagai envisages a progressive autonomous Africa, Beneatha's reaction is cynical and she, on the other hand, predicts the future emergence of neo-colonial African regimes. . . . Years later, Beneatha (Hansberry) was proven right. Africa has had more than its fair share of dictatorial regimes." (40–41)

Yet, at the same time, the play endorses Africa as a place for American blacks to draw their strength from and to connect with their ancestral roots. Asagai claims that the United States can never be home to blacks, and Hansberry seems to support Asagai's views. "As modern African activist, Asagai is a revolutionary model for Beneatha, Walter, and Black America. Operating in an African-American setting, he strengthens, but does not resolve, the destabilized ancestral connection between Africans and Black Americans" (Effiong 37). Asagai suggests that some causes are worth dying for and begins to renew Beneatha's idealism: "Asagai's beliefs certainly contribute to Beneatha's transition from brittle idealist to a more tolerant human being" (Cheney 59). Beneatha, as a black American, does not have a clear-cut cultural identity. She understands the working-class plight and the language of the bourgeoisie, while she is, at least for now, ignorant of the language and customs of Africa. "In spite of what seems to be a strong longing for African values, Beneatha, like many African-Americans, is limited by how deeply she can, and, perhaps, wants to accept and relate to Africa. Her real home is America after all" (Effiong 41). When Asagai proposes to Beneatha, asking that she come with him to Africa to practice medicine, she is hopeful but does not yet make a decision, feeling "all mixed up."

After Asagai leaves, Walter comes in, frantically searching for the paper with Lindner's telephone number. Seeing her brother rekindles Beneatha's anger and cynicism: "Symbol of a Rising Class! Entrepreneur! Titan of the system." Here, Beneatha is similar to George, using her education as a form of power. Critic Rachelle S. Gold explains: "She adopts Marxist terms and French vocabulary, learned through her college classes, and uncharitably labels Walter. Wounding his feelings in order to make him feel small, Beneatha showcases her education and wears it like a crown, all the while maintaining a degree of self-righteousness and a self-satisfied attitude with her clever turns of phrase" (9).

When Mama enters with Ruth, she looks "lost, vague, trying to catch hold, to make some sense of her former command of the world, but it eludes her." When she goes over to her plant, she seems to regain her thoughts. She fears now that she has always "aimed too high" and suggests they give up their dream and make do with the apartment. Despite Ruth's desperation—"We got to MOVE! We got to get *out of here*!!"—Mama is resigned: "I sees things differently now." Instead of moving, they will fix up the apartment: "Sometimes you just got to know when to give up some things . . . and hold on to what you got."

But Walter returns, breathless, and tells his family, "We going to do business" with Karl Lindner. Walter reveals his plan to accept Lindner's offer to pay them not to move in. Like Willy, Walter will lie and humiliate himself, if necessary, in order to find success. Mama is heartbroken: "You making something inside me cry, son. Some awful pain inside me," and she fears her son has lost his soul: "We ain't never been that—dead inside," she says, but Beneatha responds, "Well—we are dead now. All the talk about dreams and sunlight that goes on in this house. It's all dead now." But for Walter, there is still a way out; in order to get the money, he will put on a show that the white man will understand. Walter rehearses an exaggerated servility, imitating the stereotype of a black male servant, "Groveling and grinning and wringing his hands in . . . imitation of the slow-witted movie stereotype," he says, "A-hee-hee-hee! Oh, yassuh boss! Yasssssuh! Great white—" The women watch "in frozen horror."

Beneatha considers her brother as a fallen figure who cannot be redeemed: "There is nothing left to love." But Mama disagrees. In one of the play's most moving and famous speeches, Mama argues, "There is *always* something left to love. And if you ain't learned that, you ain't learned nothing." She tells her daughter that she must love her brother, especially when he is downtrodden:

Have you cried for that boy today? . . . I mean for him; what he been through and what it done to him. Child, when do you think is the time to love somebody the most? When they done good and made things easy for everybody? Well then, you ain't through learning— because that ain't the time at all. It's when he's at his lowest and can't believe in hisself 'cause the world done whipped him so! When you starts measuring somebody, measure him right, child, measure him right.

When Lindner arrives, Mama tells Walter that he must conduct his business in front of Travis and "make him understand what you doing, Walter Lee. You teach him good. Like Willy Harris taught you. You show where our five generations done come to." Moved by Mama's words about black and familial pride, Walter begins hesitantly but then eloquently tells Lindner about the family's hard work, affirming the worth of the Younger family and their right to move into any neighborhood: "And we have decided to move into our house because my father—my father—he earned it for us brick by brick."

Walter now has a more realistic and mature vision of what independence means. Though he almost resorted to accepting Lindner's offer, his family convinces him they have worked too hard to vacate their hope for advancement. His pride and humanity are more important than money and success. The events of the play serve as a rite of passage for Walter, who endures the challenges in order to arrive at a more mature understanding. Hansberry presents Walter as a strong man; he is flawed but overcomes many of his weaknesses, including greed and materialism.

Once Lindner leaves, Ruth is ecstatic, shouting "LET'S GET THE HELL OUT OF HERE!" Suddenly, everyone is bustling and happy. The last act begins in despair, but the Youngers regain hope and motivation. Walter rediscovers his dignity, and, as Mama observes, "He finally come into his manhood today, didn't he? Kind of like a rainbow after the rain." By standing up to Lindner, quietly and firmly refusing to sell out, he evolves as a man. In questioning and defining black masculinity, Hansberry situates the black woman as a part of the process. Critic Margaret B. Wilkerson posits: "Walter speaks the words and takes the action, but Mama provides the context. She, who embodies the race's will to transcend and who forms that critical link between the past and the future, articulates and transmits the traditions of the race to the next generation" (10). Wilkerson also draws a strong parallel between Mama's support of Walter and Asagai's love for Africa and his people:

> Thus in a parallel action, Asagai affirms Mama's loving support of Walter by restating her position in the sociopolitical terms of African freedom struggles. While Mama may seem to be merely conservative, clinging to an older generation, it is she who, in fact, is the mother of revolutionaries; it is she who makes possible the change and movement of the new generation. (10)

Furthermore, a parallel is also drawn between the struggle for African independence and Walter's struggle. It is symbolic then that, at the end, Walter achieves his independence without money.

The play ends with Mama alone in the apartment, "her plant on the table before her as the lights start to come down." While her children's dreams are incomplete, they have achieved happiness, and Mama has at last realized her dream of moving. As matriarch and oldest, she is testament to the potential of dreams; she has lived to see the fulfillment of the dream she and her husband first gave life to. The ending also serves as an affirmation of the Youngers' heritage, values, and independence.

The play builds to a crescendo, with an expected happy ending, although not entirely happy, as it is understood the Youngers will face racism in their new neighborhood. With little money, the Youngers will continue to be underpaid and overworked, and now they will have to endure the prejudices of a hostile neighborhood. Lloyd W. Brown analyzes the realistic complexity of the meaning of the play's ending:

In other words, the integration which is eventually realized at the end of the play has been severe, and realistically, limited by Hansberry's awareness of the contradiction between the dream ideals of reconciliation and equality, and the social realities of hatred and unresolved conflict. So without debunking the integrationist ideal, Hansberry confirms the inexorable barriers and the frustrations represented by her dominant raisin symbol. (244)

Mama pauses on her way out to show respect and appreciation for the hard work that went into making the dream come true. Her husband lingers in her memory, and, despite the struggles ahead, she seems to believe that her children will have solid futures. She takes one last look, then exits as the lights dim. Then the door opens, and she comes back for her plant, a symbol of life and survival that, "like the family, is still scraggly, but there is hope that it will flourish when cultivated in new soil" (Kennsyer 144). The final scene shows the maturation of each character, including Mama, who learns by teaching when she tells Beneatha that the true test of love is the ability to love a person when he is at his lowest. In the conclusion, the Youngers have chosen dignity and justice over fear and materialism.

Works Cited

Baraka, Amiri. "*A Raisin in the Sun*'s Enduring Passion." From *A Raisin in the Sun and The Sign in Sidney Brustein's Window*. Robert Nemiroff, ed. New York: Vintage Books, 1986.

Brown, Lloyd W. "Lorraine Hansberry as Ironist: A Reappraisal of *A Raisin in the Sun*." *Journal of Black Studies* 4, no. 3 (March 1974): 237–247.

Cheney, Anne. *Lorraine Hansberry*. Boston: Twayne, 1984.

Effiong, Philip Uko. "Realistic, Mythic, Idealistic: Hansberry and the African Image." From *In Search of a Model for African-American Drama*. Lanham, MD: University Press of America, 2000: 35–42.

Gold, Rachelle S. "'Education has spoiled many a good plow hand': How Beneatha's Knowledge Functions in *A Raisin in the Sun*." From *Reading Contemporary African American Drama*. Trudier Harris, ed. New York: Peter Lang Publishing, 2007: 1–20.

Harris, Trudier. "*A Raisin in the Sun*: The Strong Black Woman as Acceptable Tyrant." From *Saints, Sinners, Saviors: Strong Black*

Women in African American Literature. New York: Palgrave, 2001: 21–39.

Keyssar, Helene. "Sounding the Rumble of Dreams Deferred: Lorraine Hansberry's *A Raisin in the Sun*." From *The Curtain and the Veil: Strategies in Black Drama*. New York: Burt Franklin & Co., 1981: 113–146.

Wilkerson, Margaret B. "The Sighted Eyes and Feeling Heart of Lorraine Hansberry." *Black American Literature Forum* 17, no. 1: Black Theatre Issue (Spring 1983): 8–13.

Critical Views

LLOYD W. BROWN ON IRONY IN THE PLAY

The more familiar irony of the Youngers' poverty is obvious enough: their deprivations expose the gap between the American dream and the Black American reality. But, equally important, both the nature of Walter Younger's ambitions and the success of George Murchison emphasize another paradox. Ideally the promise of the American dream is aimed at the total personality of the individual: the dream is defined not only in moral terms—freedom, equality, justice, and self-realization—but also in material and socioeconomic terms. However, in practice, the moral ideals of the dream are invariably subordinated to material criteria and ambitions. Hence the socioeconomic advantages of the affluent society have been culturally ennobled as the passport to spiritual fulfillment, in much the same way that the physical freedom of the slave is a prerequisite for the total realization of human dignity.

The dialectical materialism in which the American dream is rooted in the very staple of the society's cultural modes—as in the television commercials and billboard advertisements in which toothpaste, automobiles, or deodorants promise emotional and sexual fulfillment, or in which images of novelty justify built-in obsolescence by appealing to the dream ideal of inevitable change as improvement, newness as fulfillment, and modernity as achievement. And in Hansberry's play this intrinsic ambiguity of the American dream is demonstrated by the Murchison family, especially by George, whose bourgeois materialism illustrates the American propensity to confuse material achievement with the total promise of the American dream. Thus, however well intentioned, Bigsby (1965: 157) actually reduces Hansberry's social insights to the level of idealistic naivete when he assumes that she dissociates the socioeconomic issue from "the need for spiritual replenishment which can only come with a return of dignity." And when critics such as Harold Cruse dismiss *Raisin* as bourgeois soap opera, they ignore the dramatist's fundamental ambivalence toward the American dream: having affirmed her faith in the human possibilities of the dream by deploring its deferment in the lives of some Americans (as indicated in her title), Lorraine Hansberry underscores the moral ambiguities that are inherent in the process of actually realizing the dream, in the lives of other Americans (like the Murchisons).

Moreover, when Hansberry dwells on the deferred dreams of the poor, she heightens the ironic paradox of all these ambiguities. For in the cultural psychology of the Youngers' community (and of Langston Hughes's Harlem) the deprived and the disadvantaged are like the affluent bourgeoisie in that they, too, view materialistic achievements as self-justifying, even self-redeeming, goals. The acquisition of material things (either across the counter in legal trade, or in the "revenge" looting of urban riots) is really a means of participating vicariously in the affluent society. This vicarious participation increases in value in direct ratio to the deprived individual's role of "outsider." And Walter Younger is an outsider on two counts: he is both Black and poor. Hence Walter's unabashed obsession with the insurance money as a key to instant affluence fits the materialistic priorities of the outsider's dream. In presenting the moral conflict between the spiritual promises of the dream ideal and the frank materialism of the impoverished dreamer, Hansberry is being faithful to the cultural psychology of American poverty, and to the ironic basis of her thematic design. And, viewed in this context, the importance of the money in the Youngers' eventual choice—the purchase of a house in a white neighborhood—is not the unintentional irony that C.W.E. Bigsby condescendingly attributes to Hansberry. On the contrary, this emphasis on money as the key to moral and spiritual fulfillment is consistent with the playwright's ironic overview of the socioeconomics of the American dream ideal.

The ambiguous implications of the money are also integrated with the ironies which underlie Hansberry's treatment of ideological choices between integration or separation. The crucial factor in the presentation of these choices is the play's strong hints that the choices have already been severely limited by the negative emphasis of the "raisin" title. Given the pervasive connotations of dried up hopes and deferred dreams, then the very notion of choice, with all its attendant implications of free will, has been restricted to a set of ironically balanced alternatives. From the viewpoint of the integrationist ideal, Mama is commendable in her determination to use the insurance check to buy the house. And this choice, such as it is, offers its own advantages over Walter's crassly materialistic scheme to invest the money into a dubious liquor scheme. But if housing integration is praiseworthy on the ideal principles of the American dream, then it is difficult to accept the Younger venture into a determined and hostile neighborhood as a complete fulfillment of the dream ideal. The embittering realities of enforced housing integration in Hansberry's own family life is ample evidence that she was well aware that enforced or legal integration is rather different from the ideal concept of integration as the complete reconciliation of human beings. Once again, Hansberry has ironically juxtaposed the ideal possibilities of the dream with the limitations of the American reality. Mama's (and Walter's) moral triumph over white racists is real enough, and it is undoubtedly significant in the confirmation of Walter's self-respect. But as the humiliations and hardships of the Hansberry family demonstrated in a white Chicago neighborhood, the tactical defeat of individual racists is not, ipso facto, the destruction of racism. At best it is a self-ennobling start without the certainty of a satisfactory conclusion based on genuine reconciliation. Compassion and understanding may very well be the dominant social values espoused by *Raisin*, as Bigsby and Duprey argue. But a realistic, rather than ideologically subjective, reading of the play hardly supports their view that these qualities "transcend" (racist?) history. For it is obvious enough that compassion and understanding can only transcend conflict and division if such ideals are shared equally by all sides. And it should be equally obvious that the Youngers' new white neighbors are neither compassionate nor understanding. In other words, the integration which is eventually realized at the end of the play has been severely, and realistically, limited by Hansberry's awareness of the contradiction between the dream ideals of reconciliation and equality, and the social realities of hatred and unresolved conflict. So without debunking the integrationist ideal, Hansberry confirms the inexorable barriers and the frustrations represented by her dominant raisin symbol.

Conversely, the rebuff to Walter's liquor-store scheme is no more decisive, morally, than the triumph of Mama's integrationism. Admittedly, Walter is no businessman; and his scheme is motivated by a self-serving materialism which, as we have seen, is intrinsic to the moral and psychological ambiguities of the American dream itself. But the fact still remains that the long-term socioeconomic problems of the Younger family have not been solved by the final disposition of the money on behalf of Mama's crusade for integration and for the reclamation of (Walter's) Black manhood. The Youngers now own a house in a better (white) neighborhood, but Walter's prospects for even a moderate socioeconomic self-sufficiency remain bleak; and there have been no changes in the general economic frustrations which have left their mark on both the furnishings and Ruth Younger's features:

> the furnishings of this room were actually selected with care and love and even hope—and brought to this apartment and arranged with taste and pride.

> That was a long time ago. Now the once loved pattern of the couch upholstery has to fight to show itself from under acres of crocheted doilies and couch covers which have themselves finally come to be more important than the upholstery. And here a table or a chair has been moved to disguise the worn places in the carpet; but the carpet has fought back by showing its weariness, with depressing uniformity, elsewhere on its surface.

> Weariness has, in fact, won this room. . . . All pretenses but living itself have long since vanished from the very atmosphere of this room.

Ruth is about thirty ... it is apparent that life has been little she expected, and disappointment has already begun to hang in her face. In a few years, before thirty-five even, she will be known among her people as a "settled woman" [Hansberry, 1966: 11–12].

Despite the pride and ebullience with which the play concludes, it is difficult, even then, to escape the grim reminders of these furniture symbols in the opening scene— the more difficult because the concluding scene is dominated by the same pieces of furniture as they are transferred from the old apartment to the new house. The point is that Hansberry offers no easy promise that the old frustrations and "weariness" will be left behind, or that there will be inevitable change in terms of socioeconomic achievement and complete human reconciliation. For after we have duly acknowledged all the bourgeois excesses and the poverty-inspired expectations which encourage exclusively materialistic images of the American dream, among the Murchisons and the Youngers alike, it is still a fact that the American dream ideal seeks to fulfill both the material and spiritual needs of the human personality. And as long as material and attitudinal barriers persist there will be no complete realization of the American dream for the Youngers. What they do achieve at the end of the play is neither the transcendental social triumphs envisioned by Bigsby's integrationist ethic, nor the facile soap-opera resolutions derided by the pro-separatist Cruse. Their main achievement lies in an incipient (rather than full-blown) self-esteem; but within the ironic design of Hansberry's themes, this is still counterbalanced by the forbidding prospects for both material opportunities and social regeneration as a whole. The African student, Asagai, is really an idealistic embodiment of that kind of self-esteem, but he is far from being the mouthpiece of Hansberry's ideology, as Bigsby (1967: 161) argues. For his ringing rhetoric of optimistic self-esteem comes easily in an Africa already being swept by the now famous winds of anti-colonial change. But the uncertain future of the Youngers and the persistent "weariness" of that old furniture undercut, or qualify, this optimism in an American context. And this, surely, is the ultimate irony of the play: that moral malaise and spiritual weariness have tarnished the characteristically American optimism in dreams-for-change, change-as-improvement, and improvement-as-humanization; that despite all the hallowed myths of change and the cherished dream of ideals of human fulfillment, American society allows far less room for optimism about real change than do the despised societies of the so-called underdeveloped world.

Works Cited

Bigsby, C.W.E. (1967) *Confrontation and Commitment: A Study of Contemporary American Drama 1959–1966.* Columbia: Univ. of Missouri Press.

Cruse, H. (1968) *The Crisis of the Negro Intellectual.* New York: Apollo.

DuBois, W.E.B. (1969) *Darkwater: Voices from Within the Veil.* New York: Schocken.

Duprey, R. A. (1967) "Today's dramatists," in *American Theatre*, Volume 10 of Stratford-Upon-Avon Studies. London.

Fanon, F. (1968) *The Wretched of the Earth* (C. Farrington, trans.). New York: Black Cat.

Hansberry, L. (1966) *A Raisin in the Sun.* New York: Signet.

Hughes, L. (1959) "Harlem," p. 268 in *Selected Poems.* New York: Alfred A. Knopf.

Isaacs, H. R. (1960) "Five writers and their African ancestors." *Phylon* 21, 4: 33.

Miller, J. (1971) "Lorraine Hansberry," C.W.E. Bigsby (ed.) *Poetry and Drama*, Volume 2 of *The Black American Writer.* Baltimore: Pelican.

MARY LOUISE ANDERSON ON THE PLAY'S PORTRAYAL OF WOMEN

Novelist Simone de Beauvoir once commented, "One is not born a woman. One becomes it by an ensemble of civilization."[1] The "ensemble of civilization" acculturating the American Black woman has had dramatic effects on her role today. She is both condemned and praised by sociologists and psychologists for creating and perpetuating a matriarchal stereotype. In tracing the historical roots of the matriarchal stereotype and

60

in reading some of the social and psychological comments on matriarchy's effects, it is evident that there are common tendencies of matriarchy which can provide a definition. The Black matriarch

1. regards the Black male as undependable and is frequently responsible for his emasculation,
2. is often very religious,
3. regards mothering as one of the most important things in her life,
4. attempts to shield her children from and to prepare them to accept the prejudices of the white world.

This matriarchal stereotype is presented clearly in three plays written by famous Black playwrights. By focusing on the matriarchal stereotypes in *Raisin in the Sun*, *The Amen Corner*, and *Wine in the Wilderness*, one can gain a deeper insight into the problems and controversy of this stereotype.

Lorraine Hansberry once commented that *Raisin in the Sun* is not a "Negro play" but rather a play "about honest-to-God, believable, many-sided people who happen to be Negroes."[2] Nevertheless, it is a play about matriarchy. Mama, Mrs. Lena Younger, is a matriarch, and Ruth, her daughter-in-law, struggles with the matriarch role.

The Younger family faces a daily struggle on the southside of Chicago. Into their bleak existence come the hopes and dreams brought by the money Mama is to receive from her dead husband's insurance. Every family member has plans for the money. Although Mama would like to spend it for a new house, she realizes that by ignoring her son Walter's plea for money to invest in a liquor store venture, she has "butchered up his dreams"[3] and has contributed to his emasculation. She considers Walter and the liquor store venture undependable, but she sets aside her doubts and explains to him:

Listen to me, now. I say I been wrong, son. That I been doing to you what the rest of the world has been doing to you. Walter—what you ain't never understood is that

I ain't got nothing, don't own nothing, ain't never really wanted nothing that wasn't for you. There ain't nothing as precious to me . . . there ain't nothing worth holding on to, money, dreams, nothing else—if it means it's going to destroy my boy. (Pp. 86–87)

And she gives him the money to look after and encourages him to decide about it and to become the head of the family as he should be.

Although Ruth is not the matriarch of the family, in her relationship with Walter one can see the first trait of the matriarch. She sides often with Mama and shares Mama's basic distrust of Walter's plans and doubts his judgment. Like Mama, she is emasculating Walter and is keeping him from asserting himself as protector of the family. At the beginning of the play, when Walter wants to discuss his dreams with her, she answers him with, "Eat your eggs, they gonna be cold" (p. 21). She mothers him instead of listening to and responding to his needs.

Mama exhibits the second trait of the matriarchal stereotype. Religion is an integral part of her life. She wants her children to incorporate her religious ideals into their lives. This wish is most evident when she slaps Beneatha for saying there is no God and makes her repeat, "In my mother's house there is still God" (p. 39). When Mama is furious at Walter for losing the insurance money and is at a moment of great need, she asks God for strength. Her religion sustains her and gives her the strength to be a matriarch.

Mama possesses the absolute devotion to her family true of the matriarchal stereotype. The most important things in her life are her children. When Ruth suggests that she use the insurance money to take a trip, Mama explains that she could never spend the money on herself, but must spend it on the family. Mama decides that the best way to safeguard her family is to move them to a house where they can escape the tensions that plague them. So she makes a down-payment on a house which is "the nicest place for the least amount of money" (p. 79) and sets a sum aside for her daughter Beneatha's schooling. Mama's dreams, her reasons for existence, are her family. She quotes her late husband to Ruth, "'Seems like God didn't see fit to give the black man nothing but dreams—but He did give us children to make the dreams worthwhile'" (p. 33). Mama is willing to sacrifice anything for her family. When Mama learns that Ruth is planning to have an abortion because she is so desperate about her and Walter's existence and relationship, Mama can understand Ruth's emotions and explains to Walter, "When the world gets ugly enough—a woman will do anything for her family. *The part that's already living*" (p. 62).

Mama's plant is an ever-present reminder of her matriarchal qualities. When Mama first appears, she tends her plant, just as she tends and nurtures her children. She even says of the plant, "It expresses me" (p. 101). When she envisions her house, she thinks of a garden, a symbol communicating that the house will be the place where the family can grow and flourish in better conditions. It is fitting that her family would give her gardening tools and a gardening hat, symbolizing the tools she needs to nurture them and help their dreams grow.

Notes

1. "The Negro Woman," *Ebony*, August, 1966, p. 224.
2. C.W.E. Bigsby, *The Black American Writer, Volume II: Poetry and Drama* (Deland: Everett, Edwards Inc., 1969), p. 173.
3. Lorraine Hansberry, *Raisin in the Sun* (New York: New American Library, 1966), p. 80. Parenthetical page references are to this edition.

HELENE KEYSSAR ON HANSBERRY'S STRATEGIES AS DRAMATIST

Equally central to Hansberry's strategy, the specific characteristics of the people onstage and the problems they confront are recognizable and familiar. There is, of course, for white spectators one essential difference in the characters before them: They are all black. But this is, simply, the point. No spectator can ignore the blackness of the people onstage, but the white spectator is also led to perceive how much these people are like him and his family. The audience is drawn into the family onstage by the presentation in Act I of incidents so like those we are accustomed to in our own families, be they black or white, that we come to feel kinship with the stage family. Hansberry impresses us so consistently with our similarities to the people on stage that when, in Act II, a strange white man who is in no way connected to the family enters the room, he is an intruder to white spectators as well as to black spectators and those onstage.

Nor does Hansberry rest with showing likenesses. The black characters onstage not only arouse empathy through the ordinariness of their problems and behaviors, they are often admirable and, more frequently, witty and funny. The Youngers relieve anxieties in white spectators and reaffirm self-respect in black spectators, but they also delight and interest their entire audience. *A Raisin in the Sun* resists classification as a comedy or farce because of its persistently somber undertone and the frequent proximity of events to tragic resolution, but Hansberry does skillfully and consistently use humor as a kind of insurance for the success of her intention: The laughter that the dialogue incites is more frequently with the Youngers than at them. That laughter insures that we will like these people, that we will find their presence before us pleasing. If the white audience can find the Youngers pleasing in the theater, they may then accept them in their neighborhoods and schools. Each moment of the play not only amuses us or holds us in suspense, it also provides a stone that when laid beside or above all the others, will seem to make a firm wall for a house we can imagine inhabiting. . . .

Scene III of Act II introduces a new strategic element. It sets us up for a long, ironic fall through the display of Ruth's new contentment and her dreams for the future. Ruth is happily packing for the move; she shows Beneatha curtains she has bought for the new house; she tells her sister-in-law with beaming serenity of how Walter and she went to the movies the previous night for the first time in a long time, of how they even held hands. Walter enters. His mood, though more boisterous, matches his wife's obvious joy. We cannot help but feel pleasure in their happiness.

We do not wait long before a shadow appears to dim the good cheer. The introduction of the play's only white character is set up with humor and deliberately ironic juxtaposition. Only a moment before the doorbell rings, Walter is imitating Beneatha, suggesting that at some future time she will be leaning over a patient on the operating table, asking, "By the way, what are your views on civil rights down there?" They laugh and we laugh as Beneatha goes to the door to allow the surprising entrance of a middle-aged white man in business attire. Walter immediately moves forward to confront the situation with an air of authority that amuses the women. The white man introduces himself as Karl Lindner, chairman of a "sort of welcoming committee" from the neighborhood into which the Youngers are about to move. Lindner's verbal and physical awkwardness and the deliberate vagueness of his language warn the audience from the start that this man's intentions are suspect, but only Beneatha among the characters onstage seems immediately wary of this "friendly" white man. Lindner never faces the question of race directly, but piles one ambiguous and euphemistic statement onto the next, using one rhetorical device after another, in an attempt to gain the trust of his onstage audience; by the time he gets to his point, we know he carries a message of rejection, not welcome. Lindner has come to the Youngers to buy their new house from them at a profit for the family in order to keep black people out of the neighborhood. Hansberry makes Lindner's presentation of his mission dramatically ironic because everything we have seen of the Younger family defeats the "rational" core of Lindner's argument. His central point is that people are happier when they live in a community in which the residents share a "common background," and from his viewpoint, "Negroes" and whites obviously do not have that common background. But just before he articulates this conclusion, Hansberry has Lindner describe his community in a way that for the audience should clearly appear as a striking parallel to what it knows of the behavior and desires of the Youngers: "They're not rich and fancy people; just hardworking, honest people who don't really have much but those little homes and a dream of the kind of community they want to raise their children in" (p. 407). We might laugh at how well Lindner disproved his own point about "differences in background" were it not for the fact that his bigotry will harm others, will create pain and difficulty for people like the Youngers.

Walter and Beneatha are appropriately outraged. They firmly evict the man from the house. Even if the white spectator had privately shared Lindner's rationalized prejudices, Lindner's conniving dishonesty should provoke disgust at his behavior and applause for Walter's unhesitant refusal. Here, black spectators might feel fear for the Youngers, since black spectators would know what whites have done to the homes of blacks who have moved into white neighborhoods. Hansberry's purpose, however, seems less to arouse fear in black spectators than to provoke a recognition in white spectators. The white audience needs to *see* Lindner to know he is despicable; the black audience may have assumed that possibility.

The triumph of this scene is extended and relieved when Mama returns and is told of the event. Because the Youngers respond with humor rather than bitterness to Lindner's proposal, the audience can remain empathetic rather than pitying or ashamed. Through irony, parody, and exaggeration, Ruth, Walter, and Beneatha point out the absurdity of the segregationist position. They also note so openly and unthreateningly the fears of white people that such fears are reduced to foolishness. Even the white person's worst fear is articulated in the context of a joke:

> BENEATHA: What do they think we are going to do—
>   eat 'em?
> RUTH: No, honey, marry 'em.
> MAMA (shaking her head): Lord, Lord, Lord.
> RUTH: Well—that's the way the crackers crumble. Joke.
>   [p. 409]

The jovial mood continues, both for characters and audience, as Mama is presented with gifts of gardening tools and, from Travis, an extraordinarily elaborate gardening hat. Even here

Hansberry manages to reinforce congruence of values among black and white people with Beneatha's "Travis—we were trying to make Mama Mrs. Miniver—not Scarlett O'Hara."

The audience is almost brought to believe that the play can continue in this vein indefinitely, when the levity is broken once again by the sound of the door bell. Remembering what that sound brought the last time, the audience should react on cue. Walter reinforces our response with a display of sudden tension, the motivation for which is unclear, but which does serve to focus our attention on him. Our anxiety turns out to be appropriate, although its object in the stage world would not have been foreseen. The newest visitor is one of Walter's business associates, Bobo, whose frightened demeanor vividly warns the audience that this intruder brings even worse news than did the last. Bobo, like Lindner, cannot tell his story straightforwardly, but finally, in tears, he blurts that Willy, the third business partner, has vanished with all the money intended for the liquor store. Furthermore, Mama forces Walter to admit that this amount includes not only Walter's money but Beneatha's as well. As we might have vaguely suspected from Walter's earlier obsession with the liquor store venture, he never took the money to a bank but went directly to Bobo and Willy. The Youngers' first reaction is complete silence, creating discomfort for the audience. We are released from this oppressive paralysis when Mama turns to her son to beat him on the face, but Mama's final moans of memory, her recollections of how her husband killed himself with overwork to provide what has now been stolen away, can only evoke a mixture of uneasy pity and frustration in the audience.

The problem with this newest denial of a dream for the Youngers is that it provides no real enemy, no clear object of hatred on whom we can vent our anger and thus purge ourselves of anxiety and dismay. Walter has been foolish and deceitful, but since it is *he* who has been most directly exploited, our anger must be mingled with pity. Lindner is a kind of enemy, but he is not responsible for this misfortune. Willy, the third "partner," is an abstract, unknown figure, and therefore a difficult target for cathexis. . . .

On this dismal note, Walter enters with his own resolution to the problem. His cynicism, like his sister's, has increased from his experience. To the horror of the entire family, Walter has called Mr. Lindner and asked the latter to come over so that they can now negotiate the sale of the house to the white man. Any hopes we may have had that the Youngers would have a new home are dashed. If the spectator is tempted to defend Walter's action on pragmatic grounds, Mama's voice intrudes to disallow such a response: "I came from five generations of people who was slaves and sharecroppers—but ain't nobody in my family never let nobody pay 'em no money that was a way of telling us we wasn't fit to walk the earth. We ain't never been that poor. . . . We ain't never been that dead inside" (p. 426). Mama's pride and her horrified understanding of the nature of Walter's action call forth our admiration for her and our dismay and pity for Walter. Previously, Walter had made a mistake that destroyed our hopes and his for the fulfillment of the Youngers' dreams. Now we see that the result of that mistake also destroyed the man's spirit; as Mama implies, Walter's call to Lindner is a sign of death. Mama's words do not berate her son; they are an expression of human dignity that tells us what dignity is—and what it is not.

Mama's proclamation also focuses our attention on Walter. Hansberry here has her strategy under remarkable control. Throughout the play, the author has developed our concern for each of the characters as individuals and for each of their dreams and frustrations. We have been shown three different women, not "the" black woman. Yet, in subtle ways, Walter has stood particularly apart all along: He was a man surrounded by women; his lows were nearer madness and his highs nearer ecstasy than the depressions and joys of the other characters. The Younger women did not have identical dreams, but they shared a desire for some greater sense of fulfillment, of comfort and simple pleasure. None of them, however, was struggling with the loss of self-respect that has been Walter's plight. What Mama's words lead us to recognize is that Walter has been striving for dignity—just what he lost with his call to Mr. Lindner.

What we want from Walter now is that he, too, recognize the challenge in Mama's words, and that he find in them the inspiration to recapture the dignity he has lost. But Walter's defense moves him in just the opposite direction: He falls to his knees in a hysterical imitation of the slave before the white "Father." Walter's behavior is painfully self-demeaning, but, if we feel a sense of disgust or condemnation, as Beneatha does, it is Mama who again leads us to the more complicated, more appropriate response. After Beneatha has said that Walter is no longer any brother of hers, that he is a "toothless rat," and that she despises any man who would behave this way, Mama tells her, and us, how and why that rejection is wrong:

There is always something left to love. And if you ain't learned that, you ain't learned nothing. (Looking at her) Have you cried for that boy today? I don't mean for yourself and for the family 'cause we lost the money. I mean for him; what he been through and what it done to him. Child, when do you think is the time to love somebody the most; when they done good and made things easy for everybody? Well, then, you ain't through learning—because that ain't the time at all. It's when he's at his lowest and can't believe in hisself 'cause the world done whipped him so. When you starts measuring somebody, measure him right, child, measure him right. Make sure you done taken into account what hills and valleys he come through before he got to wherever he is. [pp. 427–28]

It is not difficult to find in Mama's words the "message" of the play: When we measure someone, not just Walter, but any character on the stage or any person in any world, we must measure him right. To ignore this lesson is not just to put aside Mama's somewhat didactic sermon; it is to refuse the experience of the entire play. Mama's speech should ring true to the audience, not just because we respect her or because we find a romantic appeal in this passage, but because Hansberry has so constructed her strategy that to acknowledge the world of this play necessitates a re-examination of each of our modes of "measurement." It also means that we must accept differences between characters and ambivalences within characters: to "measure right" is partially to avoid stereotyping. If, for example, we judge Ruth in her moments of hostility toward Walter, we must alter that judgment when we witness her gestures of love (the play prohibits us from labeling her the nagging wife); if we judge Mama when she is being tyrannical, we must also do so when she is generous and understanding. Furthermore, Mama reminds us that Walter is not on his knees now because he is essentially a weak and cowardly person. He is on his knees, as we have seen, because he has been through too much, because the world has "whipped him so." Because Hansberry's strategy has so persistently been an attempt to make us accept the Youngers as ordinary people like ourselves, it would be false now to expect of Walter a strength we would certainly not presume in ourselves. We cannot condemn Walter for falling after a beating. A black spectator can empathize with Walter, while a white spectator may feel shame at being part of the world that is responsible for the whipping; any spectator should recognize in Walter's experience, however, the defeat of having struggled and lost.

A Raisin in the Sun could end with Mama's speech. Such an ending would leave us with a message and a vague depression. We do not have sufficient reason to condemn Walter, but neither do we have the reasons his family has to love him and feel a deep anguish at his defeat. We have also only seen Walter rehearse his humiliation; although we have no reason to hope that he or other characters onstage will change his behavior, we would be left without a sense of completion were we not to see Walter's encounter with Lindner. Yet we feel a sense of futility when Lindner does arrive. There appears no way for the characters onstage to aid Walter or alter the situation.

There is also the important frustration in being an audience member who wishes to aid the characters on stage but cannot because one is in a world separate from theirs. When the playwright creates such an effect, the intent is that we transport the desire to change behavior, either our own or someone else's, into the world in which we do or can act. Drama presents to the audience the limits of a world and arouses the desire that someone break through those limits. In tragedy, the hero is most often thwarted in his attempts to deny or destroy the boundaries of his world, but our sorrow for him relieves us of our own impotence and allows us to act anew in our world. In *A Raisin in the Sun* we are led to the edge of tragedy, from where we can see the abyss into which Walter is falling, yet we are finally led away from that edge because Hansberry does not intend us to remove ourselves from her characters. In traditional tragedy, we are meant to see the central character or characters as other and greater than ourselves: Their falls thus create anguish; and their struggles provide hope. In *A Raisin in the Sun*, we are meant to see ourselves as like these characters in all important ways. Thus, neither pity nor awe is wholly appropriate, for the former would lead to self-pity and the latter to egotism.

More than in our experience of many plays, when we arrive at the end of *A Raisin in the Sun* we feel that everything else in the play has been set up precisely to accomplish the final scene. One reason for this sensation is that we know we are being told a story, and we expect a story to have a beginning, a middle, and an end. We have also been led to recognize that this is, in an important way, Walter's story, and his tale is not yet complete. Once engaged in the final episode, its surprising reversal and its emphatic assertion of survival tend to erase our memories of earlier troublings much as the baby that arrives after labor dissolves the memory of the pain that brought it forth.

Our attention is all on Walter as the final portion of the play begins. Walter has "set this scene," and the other Youngers, like the audience, are witnesses. Lindner, the white man from the neighborhood committee, returns to the Youngers' home expecting, as we do, that Walter is about to sell the house to the white community. Just as Hansberry has played with our curiosity in previously unpredictable scenes with Lindner and then Bobo, she now elongates Walter's response to Lindner. In words that approach a parody of Lindner's earlier speech, while sustaining an air of utter sincerity, Walter speaks slowly of his family, of his pride in his sister's studies, and with increasing emphasis, of his father. Our attention is held rapt because this is not the role Walter has rehearsed; we have no reason not to expect him eventually to come to his deal, but the words he speaks suggest a sentiment and pride we have not seen previously in Walter. We are thus only vaguely prepared for Walter's sudden reversal. Crying unashamedly in front of "the man" Walter finally says that the Youngers will move into their new house, "because my father—my father—he earned it."

With these words, Walter pays a debt both to his parents and to the audience. The time and trust they and we have invested in him are now rewarded. He is behaving with the dignity we have had only glimpses of since the beginning of the play. As he continues to speak, he affirms this trust for both black and white spectators: "We don't want to make no trouble for nobody or fight no causes—but we will try to be good neighbors." Hansberry thus reassures white spectators that the Youngers do not want to cause difficulties and reassures black spectators that the Youngers will *try* to be good neighbors but will not guarantee any particular kind of behavior.

If we contemplate Walter's sudden redemption, we will be puzzled by it. The only possible motivation we are given for Walter's change of mind is the brief appearance of Travis before Lindner's arrival. Perhaps we are to infer that the sight of his son jars Walter into understanding that it is not only he who will suffer humiliation and loss of a dream. But the script does not guide the audience to that conclusion. Rather, we are given no pause to search for an explanation of Walter's new behavior. The moment Lindner leaves, Ruth cries, "LET'S GET THE HELL OUT OF HERE!" The women become so hastily involved in other activities and conversations that they suggest that Walter's redemption is too fragile and too fortunate to be questioned. The bustle of activity at the end of the play prevents excessive sentimentality, but it also demands that the audience feel satisfaction without understanding.

If we look closer at that feeling of satisfaction, we will find in it the essence of Hansberry's strategy. We are pleased that Walter has behaved with dignity and relieved that the Youngers will go on, not in futile desperation but with a sense of a new world before them. They have not changed very much, nor did Hansberry lead the audience to demand or expect great changes. The conclusion of *A Raisin in the Sun* returns us to a world of buoyant wit, and our ability once again to share laughter with the Youngers reassures us of a shared vision of the world.

It is this very laughter, however, that prevents many spectators from perceiving the contradictions of the Youngers' world. Early in the play, our laughter relieves us from fully confronting the evidence that *A Raisin in the Sun* presents not simply the dreams of the characters but the complexities of "dreams deferred." Nor does the conclusion of the play make us ashamed of our good humor. The Youngers are back in high spirits. We can leave the theater happily persuaded that still another family has rightfully joined the infinitely extensive American middle class.

Such an experience of Hansberry's play is not a mistake; it may be what is essentially intended, but it is simply not whole. There is a confusion in the world of the Youngers, which Harold Cruse glimpses but finally misperceives: "The Younger family was carefully tidied up for its on-stage presentation. . . . There were no numbers runners in sight, no bumptious slick, young "cats" from downstairs sniffling after Mama Younger's pretty daughter on the corner, no shyster preachers hustling Mama into the fold, no fallen woman, etc."[11] Such omissions may be glaring to some spectators, but can be understood as a decision not to distract a middle-class audience from their recognition of the Youngers as similar to themselves. To gain the aura of authenticity for those who know the ghetto might mean to relinquish some contact with a middle-class audience. To untidy the Youngers might be to dishevel as well the audience's social and aesthetic security that allows it to recognize these people.

The difficulty with a genuine recognition of the world of *A Raisin in the Sun* is not that Hansberry lies to maintain order; it is rather that she is finally unable to lie. Her drama reveals more than the main intention of her strategy would wish. The

Youngers are not moving into the middle-class when they move into their new house; they are simply and only moving into a house. For many Americans, the act of purchasing one's own house clearly signifies upward mobility and membership in the middle class. This signification occurs for at least two different reasons: In order to buy a house, the purchaser must present some assurances of stable income and occupation, and the act itself is one of choice. Since the dramatic structure of *A Raisin in the Sun* can exist only because a choice does exist, we can allow ourselves to believe that we are in the world of the middle class. But choice for the Youngers is poignantly and emphatically a singular event. They are only able to make a choice because the ten thousand dollar benefit from Mr. Younger's life insurance policy has suddenly appeared in their mailbox. Ironically, it is through death, not the nature of their lives, that they are able to choose to buy a house.

It is made amply clear that Hansberry cannot lie about the limitations of this move for the Youngers. Ruth recognizes fully that she will have to work herself to the bone to help keep up the mortgage payment, yet the early scenes of the play remind us that she cannot continue her pregnancy in health and harmony with her domestic work. And what will happen when Ruth does have a baby? If the implied assumption is that Mama will take over the rearing of another Younger child, this must also be an assumption of further internal destruction in the family, since the tensions caused by Mama's meddling in Travis's upbringing have been poignantly demonstrated. Walter Lee's situation is at least equally closed. Not only are there no new options for him to change his occupation, for him to find work less servile than that of a chauffeur, but the dream of going into business for himself has itself been muddied. The theft of his share of the insurance policy concretely removes his chance for starting a liquor business now, but it also suggests that ventures into the world of private business necessitate a kind of cunning, distrust, and encounter with corruption that calls the entire operation into question.

To turn to Beneatha or Travis only further reveals the imprisonment of the family. Beneatha may be able at the end of the play to return to her fantasies of getting married and going off to practice medicine in Africa, but the audience, at least, should remember that such notions are now even more fantastic than before, because Walter Lee has lost not only the money for his business but Beneatha's money for school. Travis may now have a room of his own, at least until the arrival of the new baby, but how will the family find the fifty cents (if it is only fifty cents out in the white suburbs) for school activities when there is no new income and the pressures of taking care of the house will create even greater financial burdens? If Travis's own parents did not like the image of their son picking up extra money by carrying bags at the supermarket, how will the new white middle-class neighbors respond to the black boy who totes packages for a few pennies after school? The bustle of moving may allow all members of the family to repress momentarily their fears and despair, but Beneatha's earlier words to Asagai, her African friend, are the only authentic description of where the family really finds itself: "Don't you see there isn't any real progress, Asagai, there is only one large circle that we march in, around and around, each of us our own little picture—in front of us—our own little mirage which we think is the future" (p. 419).

Hansberry has succeeded in persuading the audience to the legitimacy of the Youngers' aspirations, but she has simultaneously shown the extreme difficulty, if not impossibility, for this family of fulfilling their dreams of change, stability, and comfort. Hansberry directly undercuts the central middle-class American notion of "equality of opportunity" by presenting the white man, Mr. Lindner, who finally believes that opportunities for blacks should not be identical with those for whites, that blacks should not move into a white neighborhood; this is only one direct instance, however, of the limitations of opportunity for the Youngers. Mr. Lindner slams a door on the Youngers that may have appeared to have been open; other doors for the Youngers simply remain closed.

Perhaps despite her intentions, Hansberry's play takes one additional step to undermine a belief in one great middle-class world for all Americans: At crucial moments her characterizations and plot structure call into question the very nature of the values and opportunities being presented as shared.

> BENEATHA (hissingly): Yes just look at what the New World hath wrought! . . . There he is! *Monsieur le petit bourgeois noir*—himself! There he is! Symbol of a Rising Class! Entrepreneur! Titan of the system!
> . . . I look at you and I see the final triumph of stupidity in the world! [p. 472]

Walter's subsequent courage in rejecting Mr. Lindner's bribe prevents us from concluding that Walter is "the final triumph of stupidity in the world." But while we may be forced away from this particular conclusion, the first lines of Beneatha's attack may resound with accuracy. The world of *A Raisin in the Sun* is often affable, but the assaults on class identity for black people suggest a paradoxically coherent confusion.[12]

That recognition may lead to at least small changes in the social and political worlds from which the audience comes. Woodie King and Ron Milner, strong contemporary proponents of a black theater, have urged in the introduction to their anthology of black drama that "*A Raisin in the Sun* reaffirmed in blacks the necessity for more involvement in black theater."[13] Partially by the inclusion in its casts of such notable black theater artists as Lonne Elder III, Robert Hooks, Douglas Turner Ward, and Ossie Davis, the play "marked a turning point."[14] These remarks emphasize the play as historical event rather than experience for an audience. It may well be that this is how *A Raisin in the Sun* will be best remembered, but the fact that it is remembered is inseparable from the play's ability to impress an audience. That impression may not have been as facile as it once appeared. *A Raisin in the Sun*'s success raised the curtain for many subsequent productions of black theater; it may also have lifted the veil for some spectators to glimpse the complexity of black life in America. Even for black spectators who know that complexity in their daily lives, the act of witnessing its revelation, with all of the play's omissions and inconsistencies, can be important.

76

At the end of *A Raisin in the Sun*, Mama starts to leave, then symbolically returns for her plant. The plant, like the family, is still scraggly, but there is hope that it will flourish when cultivated in new soil. Although Hansberry wanted us to see that plant as representing the Younger family, some twenty years later it also suggests the place *A Raisin in the Sun* has found in the evolution of black drama.

Notes

11. Cruse, p. 280.

12. The case I have been making here, both for and against Hansberry and *A Raisin in the Sun*, is not far removed from the case made by Georg Lukács in his discussion of Balzac. Lukács summarizes his argument at the beginning of the essay "Balzac: The Peasants," in *Studies in European Realism* (New York: Grosset & Dunlap, 1964), saying, "Yet, for all his painstaking preparation and careful planning, what Balzac really did in this novel was the exact opposite of what he had set out to do: what he depicted was not the tragedy of the aristocratic estate but of the peasant smallholding." But Hansberry is finally neither as historically accurate nor as deserving of the kind of praise that Lukács gives Balzac. Hers is not precisely the same case, because it is never clear that she knows what she is revealing. Like Balzac, she provides no solutions, but unlike Balzac, she tends to disguise the space within which she raises questions. This is not a matter of mendacity, but neither is it an instance of the insight of genius revealing itself despite itself.

13. Woodie King and Ron Milner, "Evolution of a People's Theater," in *Black Drama Anthology* (New York: Columbia University Press, 1971), p. vii.

14. *Ibid.*

MARGARET B. WILKERSON ON THE PLAY'S SOCIOPOLITICAL ELEMENTS

As a black writer, Hansberry was caught in a paradox of expectations. She was expected to write about that which she "knew best," the black experience, and yet that expression was doomed to be called parochial and narrow. Hansberry, however, challenged these facile categories and forced a redefinition of the term "universality," one which would include the dissonant voice of an oppressed American minority. As a young college student, she had wandered into a rehearsal of Sean O'Casey's *Juno and the Paycock*. Hearing in the wails and moans of the Irish characters a universal cry of human misery, she determined to capture that sound in the idiom of her own people—so that it could be heard by all. "One of the most sound ideas in dramatic writing," she would later conclude, "is that in order to create the universal, you must pay very great attention to the specific. Universality, I think, emerges from truthful identity of what is. . . . In other words, I think people, to the extent we accept them and believe them as who they're supposed to be, to that extent they can become everybody."[3] Such a choice by a black writer posed an unusual challenge to the literary establishment and a divided society ill-prepared to comprehend its meaning.

"All art is ultimately social: that which agitates and that which prepares the mind for slumber," Hansberry argued, attacking another basic tenet held by traditional critics. One of the most fundamental illusions of her time and culture, she believed, is the idea that art is not and should not make a social statement. The belief in "l'art pour l'art" permeates literary and theatrical criticism, denying the integral relationship between society and art. "The writer is deceived who thinks he has some other choice. The question is not whether one will make a social statement in one's work—but only *what* the statement will say, for if it says anything at all, it will be social."[4]

It would have been impossible for a person of her background and sensitivity to divorce herself from the momentous social events of the 1950s and 1960s. This period witnessed the beginning of a Cold War between the U.S. and Russian superpowers, a rising demand by blacks for civil rights at home, and a growing intransigence by colonized peoples throughout the world. Isolation is the enemy of black writers, Hansberry believed; they are obligated to participate in the intellectual and social affairs of humankind everywhere.

In a 1959 speech to young writers, she explained the impact of social and political events on her world view:

I was born on the South Side of Chicago. I was born black and a female. I was born in a depression after one world war, and came into my adolescence during another. While I was still in my teens the first atom bombs were dropped on human beings at Nagasaki and Hiroshima. And by the time I was twenty-three years old, my government and that of the Soviet Union had entered actively into the worst conflict of nerves in human history—the Cold War.

I have lost friends and relatives through cancer, lynching and war. I have been personally the victim of physical attack which was the offspring of racial and political hysteria. I have worked with the handicapped and seen the ravages of congenital diseases that we have not yet conquered, because we spend our time and ingenuity in far less purposeful wars; I have known persons afflicted with drug addiction and alcoholism and mental illness. I see daily on the streets of New York, street gangs and prostitutes and beggars. I have, like all of you, on a thousand occasions seen indescribable displays of man's very real inhumanity to man, and I have come to maturity, as we all must, knowing that greed and malice and indifference to human misery and bigotry and corruption, brutality, and perhaps above all else, ignorance—the prime ancient and persistent enemy of man—abound in this world. I say all of this to say that one cannot live with sighted eyes and feeling heart and not know and react to the miseries which afflict this world.[5]

Hansberry's "sighted eyes" forced her to confront fully the depravity, cruelty, and utter foolishness of men's actions, but her "feeling heart" would not allow her to lose faith in humanity's potential for overcoming its own barbarity. This strong and uncompromising belief in the future of humankind informed her plays and sometimes infuriated her critics.

Her best-known play, *A Raisin in the Sun*, dramatizes the seductiveness of American materialistic values. The title and theme are taken from a Langston Hughes poem, "Harlem," which asks: "What happens to a dream deferred?"[6] The dreams of the Youngers, a black family living in South-Side Chicago, have gone unfulfilled too long. Their hopes of enjoying the fruits of freedom and equality have been postponed as they struggled merely to survive economically. Into this setting comes $10,000 insurance money paid upon the death of Walter Younger, Sr. Lena Younger (Mama) and her adult son Walter clash over the money's use. Mama wants to save some for her daughter Beneatha's college education and to make a down payment on a new house in order to get the family out of the cramped quarters and shared bathroom of their tiny apartment. Walter wants to invest in a liquor store. They share the dream of improving the family's situation, but Walter, consumed with the frustrations of his dead-end chauffeur's job, believes that the money itself is synonymous with life. The possession of money and the things it can buy will make him a man in the eyes of his family and society, he asserts.

The intrusion of American cultural values is evident both in this tug of war and in the character of Lena. Mama, who initially fits the popular stereotype of the Black Mammy, seems to be the domineering head of household. She rules everyone's life, even making a down payment on a house in an all-white neighborhood without consulting her son. However, as she begins to comprehend the destructive effect of her actions on Walter, she relinquishes her authority and gives him the balance of the money to invest as he wishes. Walter's elation is short-lived, however, because he loses the money by entrusting it to his "partner," a slick con man who disappears. In an effort to recover his loss, Walter tells his family that he will accept money from his prospective neighbors who would rather buy him off than live next door to him. The decision is a personal test for Walter, for he is sorely tempted to sacrifice his pride and integrity for mercenary values: "There ain't no causes—there ain't nothing but taking in this world and he who takes most is smartest—and it don't make a damn bit of difference *how*."[7] In a highly dramatic moment, Walter gets down on his knees and shows his mother how he will beg, if necessary, for the white man's money—scratching his head and laughing in the style of the old Uncle Tom. Even with this display, Mama does not berate him, but rather surrounds him with her circle of love and compassion, saying to the others who have witnessed this scene:

> Have you cried for that boy today? I don't mean for yourself and for the family 'cause we lost the money. I mean for him; what he been through and what it done to him. Child, when do you think is the time to love somebody the most; when they done good and made things easy for everybody? ... that ain't the time at all. It's when he's at his lowest and can't believe in hisself 'cause the world done whipped him so. When you starts measuring somebody, measure him right, child, measure him right. Make sure you done taken into account what hills and valleys he come through before he got to wherever he is.[8]

Just as the stereotyped image of the Mammy gives way to the caring, understanding mother, historic cornerstone of the black family, so the materialism of Walter crumbles before his reaffirmation of traditional values of pride and selfhood. He tells the baffled representative of the hostile white community that he and his family will move into their house because his father and the generations before him earned that right. Walter speaks the words and takes the action, but Mama provides the context. She, who embodies the race's will to transcend and who forms that critical link between the past and the future, articulates and transmits the traditions of the race to the next generation. Her wisdom and compassion provide the context for him to attain true manhood, to advance materially without becoming materialistic.

The story of the Younger family is the story of a struggle to retain human values and integrity while forcing change in a society where human worth is measured by the dollar. Through the supporting character Asagai, an African intellectual, the personal dynamics of that struggle become a microcosm of the struggle for liberation throughout the world and especially in

Africa. Hansberry achieves this connection through Asagai's response to Walter's foolish mistake. He warns the disappointed Beneatha that she is using her brother's error as an excuse to give up on "the ailing human race" and her own participation in it. Beneatha argues that Walter's action is no different from the pettiness, ignorance, and foolishness of other men who turn idealistic notions of freedom and independence into absurd dreams. But Asagai reacts vehemently, proclaiming that one mistake does not stop a movement. Others will correct that mistake and go on, probably to make errors of their own—but the result, however halting, is movement, change, and advancement forward.[9] Thus, in a parallel action, Asagai affirms Mama's loving support of Walter by restating her position in the sociopolitical terms of African freedom struggles. While Mama may seem to be merely conservative, clinging to an older generation, it is she who, in fact, is the mother of revolutionaries; it is she who makes possible the change and movement of the new generation.

Despite Mama's importance to the theme, Walter remains a worthy and unique counterpoint. In his own way, Walter signals the wave of the future. He is restless, hungry, angry—a victim of his circumstance but at the same time the descendant of his proud forebears, struggling to transcend his victimhood. When he, in a drunken flare, leaps onto a table and assumes the stance of an African chieftain, he unconsciously embodies that proud and revolutionary spirit which is his heritage. When he quietly refuses the white citizens' payoff at the end of the play, he becomes the symbolic father of the aggressive, articulate black characters who would stride the boards in the 1960s. Indeed, Walter, who has begun to shed the materialism of the majority culture, leads the march to a different drum.

Testimony to Hansberry's craftsmanship is the fact that these complex themes and perceptions are presented unobtrusively, emerging naturally as a result of action and dialogue. A master of heightened realism, she carefully orchestrates the moods of the play, using highly symbolic, nonrealistic actions when needed and guiding both performer and audience through a maze of emotional and humorous moments. The play makes a social statement, but not at the expense of its ability to engage. In fact, the miracle of this popular play is that Hansberry successfully involves her audience, whether white or black, in a complete identification and support for the struggles of this family.

Notes

3. Lorraine Hansberry, *To Be Young, Gifted and Black: Lorraine Hansberry in Her own Words*, adapted by Robert Nemiroff (New York: New American Library, 1970), p. 128.

4. Lorraine Hansberry, "The Negro Writer and His Roots: Toward a New Romanticism," a speech delivered to the Black Writers' Conference, Henry Hudson Hotel, New York City, 1 Mar. 1959, pp. 5–6.

5. Ibid., p. 41.

6. In *Selected Poems* (New York: Knopf, 1974), p. 268.

7. Lorraine Hansberry, *A Raisin in the Sun/The Sign in Sidney Brustein's Window* (New York: New American Library, 1966), p. 122.

8. Ibid., p. 125.

9. Ibid., pp. 114–16.

AMIRI BARAKA ON REALISM IN THE PLAY

When *Raisin* first appeared in 1959, the Civil Rights Movement was in its earlier stages. And as a document reflecting the *essence* of those struggles, the play is unexcelled. For many of us it was—and remains—the quintessential civil rights drama. But any attempt to confine the play to an era, a mind-set, an issue ("Housing") or set of topical concerns was, as we now see, a mistake. The truth is that Hansberry's dramatic skills have yet to be properly appreciated—and not just by those guardians of the status quo who pass themselves off as dramatic critics. For black theater artists and would-be theorists especially, this is ironic because the play is probably the most widely appreciated— particularly by African Americans—black drama that we have.

Raisin lives in large measure because black people have kept it alive. And because Hansberry has done *more* than document, which is the most limited form of realism. She is a *critical realist*, in a way that Langston Hughes, Richard Wright, and Margaret Walker are. That is, she *analyzes* and *assesses* reality and shapes her statement as an aesthetically powerful and politically advanced work of art. Her statement cannot be separated from the characters she creates to embody, in their totality, the life she observes: it becomes, in short, the living material of the work, part of its breathing body, integral and alive.

George Thompson in *Poetry and Marxism* points out that drama is the most expressive artistic form to emerge out of great social transformation. Shakespeare is the artist of the destruction of feudalism—and the emergence of capitalism. The mad Macbeths, bestial Richard III's, and other feudal worthies are actually shown, like the whole class, as degenerate—and degenerating. This is also why Shakespeare deals with race (*Othello*), anti-Semitism (*The Merchant of Venice*), and feminism (*The Taming of the Shrew*); because these *will be* the continuing dilemmas of the bourgeois epoch! If we—opponents of racism, sexism, and the degeneracies of capitalism today—were to write Richard the Nix and Ronnie the Rex, we would not be called the Bard's heirs, although it is the bourgeoisie who came to shower celebration on Shakespeare—now they provide sterile, dead productions to hide the real texts.

Hansberry's play, too, was political agitation. It dealt with the very same issues of democratic rights and equality that were being aired in the streets. It dealt with them with an unabating dramatic force, vision, political concreteness and clarity that, in retrospect, are awesome. But it dealt with them not as abstractions, fit only for infantile-left pamphlets, but as they are *lived*. In reality.

All of *Raisin's* characters speak *to* the text and are critical to its dramatic tensions and understanding. They are necessarily larger than life—in impact—but crafted meticulously from living social material. . . .

A Raisin in the Sun is about *dreams*, ironically enough. And how those psychological projections of human life can come into conflict like any other product of that life. For Lena, a new house, the stability and happiness of her children, are her principal dream. And as such this is the completion of a dream she and her late husband—who has literally, like the slaves, been *worked* to death—conceived together.

Ruth's dream, as mother and wife, is somewhat similar. A room for her son, an inside toilet. She dreams as one of those triply oppressed by society—as worker, as African American, and as woman. But her dream, and her mother-in-law's, conflicts with Walter Lee's. He is the chauffeur to a rich white man and dreams of owning all and doing all the things he sees "Mr. Arnold" do and own. On one level Walter Lee is merely aspiring to full and acknowledged humanity; on another level he yearns to strut his "manhood," a predictable mix of *machismo* and fantasy.

But Hansberry takes it even further to show us that on still another level Walter Lee, worker though he be, has the "realizable" dream of the black petty bourgeoisie. "There he is! *Monsieur le petit bourgeois noir*—himself!" cries Beneatha, the other of Lena Younger's children. "There he is—Symbol of a Rising Class! Entrepreneur! Titan of the system!" The deepness of this is that Hansberry can see that the conflict of dreams is not just that of individuals but, more importantly, of classes. Not since Theodore Ward's *Big White Fog* (1938) has there been a play so thoroughly and expertly reflective of class struggle within a black family.

Beneatha dreams of medical school. She is already socially mobile, finding a place, as her family cannot, among other petty bourgeois aspirants on the rungs of "education," where their hard work has put her. Her aspiration is less caustic, more attainable than Walter's. But she yearns for something more. Her name Beneatha (as who ain't?) should instruct us. She is, on the one hand, secure in the collegiate world of "ideas" and elitism, above the mass; on the other, undeceived by the myths and symbols of class and status. Part militant, part dilettante, "liberated" woman, little girl, she questions everything and dreams of service to humanity, an identity beyond self and family in the liberation struggles of her people. Ah, but will she have the strength to stay the course?

Hansberry has Beneatha grappling with key controversies of the period, but also some that had yet to clearly surface. And she grapples with some that will remain with us until society itself is changed: The relationship of the intellectual to the masses. The relationship of African Americans to Africans. The liberation movement itself and the gnawing necessity of black self-respect in its many guises (e.g., "straightened" hair vs. "the natural"). Written in 1956 and first seen by audiences in the new revivals, the part of the text in which Beneatha unveils her hair—the "perm" cut off and she glowing with her original woolly crown—precedes the "Afro" by a decade. Dialogue between Beneatha and her mother, brother, Asagai and George Murchison digs into all these still-burning concerns.

Similarly, Walter Lee and Ruth's dialogues lay out his male chauvinism and even self- and group-hate born of the frustration of too many dreams too long deferred: the powerlessness of black people to control their own fate or that of their families in capitalist America where race is place, white is right, and money makes and defines the man. Walter dreams of using his father's insurance money to buy a liquor store. This dream is in conflict not only with the dreams of the Younger women, but with reality. But Walter appreciates only his differences with—and blames—the women. Throughout the work, Hansberry addresses herself to issues that the very young might feel only *The Color Purple* has raised. Walter's relationship to his wife and sister, and Beneatha's with George and Asagai, gives us a variety of male chauvinism—working class, petty bourgeois, African.

Asagai, the Nigerian student who courts Beneatha, dreams of the liberation of Africa and even of taking Beneatha there: "We will pretend that . . . you have only been away for a day." But that's not reality either, though his discussion of the dynamics and dialectics of revolution—and of the continuity of human struggle, the only means of progress—still rings with truth!

Hansberry's warnings about neo-colonialism and the growth (and corruption) of a post-colonial African bourgeoisie—"the servants of empire," as Asagai calls them—are dazzling because of their subsequent replication by reality. As is, above all, her sense of the pressures mounting inexorably in this one typical household, and in Walter Lee especially, and of where they must surely lead. It was the "explosion" Langston Hughes talked about in his great poem "Harlem"—centerpiece of his incomparable *Montage of a Dream Deferred*, from which the play's title was taken—and it informs the play as its twinned projection: dream or coming reality.

These are the categories Langston proposes for the dream:

Does it dry up
Like a raisin in the sun?

Dried up is what Walter Lee and Ruth's marriage had become, because their respective dreams have been deferred. When Mama Lena and Beneatha are felled by news of Walter Lee's weakness and dishonesty, their life's will—the desired greening of their humanity—is defoliated.

Or fester like a sore—
And then run?

Walter Lee's dream has festered, and in his dealings with the slack-jawed con man Willie (merchant of the stuff of dreams), his dream is "running."

We speak of the American Dream. Malcolm X said that for the Afro-American it was the American Nightmare. The little ferret man (played again tellingly by John Fiedler, one of the original cast on Broadway and in the film) is the dream's messenger, and the only white person in the play. His name is Lindner (as in "neither a borrower nor a Lindner be"), and the thirty or so "pieces of silver" he proffers are meant to help the niggers understand the dichotomous dream.

"But you've got to admit that a man, right or wrong, has the right to want to have the neighborhood he lives in a certain kind of way," says Lindner. Except black folks. Yes, these "not rich and fancy" representatives of white lower-middle America have a dream, too. A class dream, though it does not even serve them. But they are kept ignorant enough not to understand that the real dimensions of that dream—white supremacy, black "inferiority," and with them ultimately, though they know it not, fascism and war—are revealed every day throughout the world as deadly to human life and development—even their own.

In the post–civil rights era, in "polite" society, theirs is a dream too gross even to speak of *directly* anymore. And this is another legacy of the play: It was one of the shots fired (and still being fired) at the aberrant white-supremacy dream that is American reality. And the play is also a summation of those shots, that battle, its heightened statement. Yet the man, Lindner, explains him/them self, and there is even a hint of compassion for Lindner the man as he bumbles on in outrageous innocence of all he is actually saying—that "innocence" for which Americans are famous, which begs you to love and understand me for hating you, the innocence that kills. Through him we see this other dream:

> Does it stink like rotten meat?
> Or crust and sugar over—
> Like a syrupy sweet?

Almost everyone else in the play would sound like Martin Luther King at the march on Washington were we to read their speeches closely and project them broadly. An exception is George Murchison (merchant's son), the "assimilated" good bourgeois whose boldest dream, if one can call it that, is to "get the grades . . . to pass the course . . . to get a degree" en route to making it the American way. George wants only to "pop" Beneatha after she, looking good, can be seen with him in the "proper" places. He is opposed to a woman's "thinking" at all, and black heritage to him "is nothing but a bunch of raggedy-ass spirituals and some grass huts." The truth of this portrait is one reason the black bourgeoisie has not created the black national theaters, publishing houses, journals, galleries, film corporations, and newspapers the African American people desperately need. So lacking in self-respect are members of this class of George's, they even let the Kentucky Colonel sell us fried chicken and giblets.

The clash between Walter Lee and George, one of the high points of class struggle in the play and a dramatic tour de force, gives us the dialogue between the *sons* of the house and of the field slaves. And Joseph Phillips' portrayal of George's dumb behind in the production I saw is so striking because he understands that George thinks he is "cool." He does not understand he is corny!

When *Raisin* appeared the movement itself was in transition, which is why Hansberry could sum up its throbbing profile with such clarity. The baton was ready to pass from "George's father" as leader of the "Freedom Movement" (when its real muscle was always the Lena Youngers and their husbands) to the Walter Lees and Beneathas and Asagais and even the Georges.

In February 1960, black students at North Carolina A & T began to "sit in" at Woolworth's in a more forceful attack on segregated public facilities. By the end of 1960, some 96,000 students across the country had gotten involved in these sit-ins. In 1961, Patrice Lumumba was assassinated, and black intellectuals and activists in New York stormed the United Nations gallery. While Ralph Bunche (George's spiritual father) shrank back "embarrassed"—probably more so than by slavery and colonialism! But the Pan African thrust had definitely returned.

And by this time, too, Malcolm X, "the fire prophet," had emerged as the truest reflector of black mass feelings. It was of someone like Malcolm that Walter Lee spoke as in a trance in prophecy while he mounts the table to deliver his liquor-fired call to arms. (Nation of Islam headquarters was Chicago where the play is set!) Walter Lee embodies the explosion to be—what happens when the dream is deferred past even the patience of the Lena Youngers.

Young militants like myself were taken with Malcolm's coming, with the imminence of explosion (e.g., Birmingham, when black Walters and Ruths struck back with ice-picks and clubs in response to the bombing of a black church and the killing of four little girls in Sunday school).

We thought Hansberry's play was part of the "passive resistance" phase of the movement, which was over the minute Malcolm's penetrating eyes and words began to charge through the media with deadly force. We thought her play "middle class" in that its focus seemed to be on "moving into white folks' neighborhoods," when most blacks were just trying to pay their rent in ghetto shacks.

We missed the essence of the work—that Hansberry had created a family on the cutting edge of the same class and ideological struggles as existed in the movement itself and among the people. What is most telling about our ignorance is that Hansberry's play still remains overwhelmingly popular and evocative of black and white reality, and the masses of black people dug it true.

The next two explosions in black drama, Baldwin's *Blues for Mr. Charlie* and my own *Dutchman* (both 1964) raise up the militancy and self-defense clamor of the movement as it came fully into the Malcolm era: Jimmy by constructing a debate between King (Meridian) and Richard (Malcolm), and I by having Clay openly advocate armed resistance. But neither of these plays is as much a statement from the African American majority as is *Raisin*. For one thing, they are both (regardless of their "power") too concerned with white people.

It is Lorraine Hansberry's play which, though it seems "conservative" in form and content to the radical petty bourgeoisie (as opposed to revolutionaries), is the accurate telling and stunning vision of the real struggle. Both Clay and Richard are rebellious scions of the middle class. The Younger family is part of the black majority, and the concerns I once dismissed as "middle class"—buying a house and moving into "white folks' neighborhoods"—are actually reflective of the essence of black people's striving and the will to defeat segregation, discrimination, and national oppression. There is no such thing as a "white folks' neighborhood" except to racists *and to those submitting to racism.*

The Younger family is the incarnation—*before* they burst from the bloody Southern backroads and the burning streets of Watts and Newark onto TV screens and the *world* stage—of our common ghetto-variety Fanny Lou Hamers, Malcolm X's, and Angela Davises. And their burden surely will be lifted, or one day it certainly will "explode."

When Lorraine Hansberry's *A Raisin in the Sun* opened on Broadway in 1959, the vast majority of white critics praised the play's "universality." One reviewer wrote, "A Negro wrote this show. It is played, with one exception, by Negroes. Half the audiences here are Negroes. Even so, it isn't written for Negroes. . . . It's a show about people, white or colored. . . . I see 'A Raisin in the Sun' as part of the general culture of the U.S."[1] The phrase "happens to be" appeared with remarkable frequency among reviews: the play was "about human beings, who happen to be Negroes"[2] (or "a family that happens to be colored"[3]); Sidney Poitier played "the angry young man who happens to be a Negro."[4]

Other white reviewers, however, praised the play not for its universality, but for its particularity. "The play is honest," wrote Brooks Atkinson, critic for the *New York Times*. "[Hansberry] has told the inner as well as the outer truth about a Negro family in the southside of Chicago at the present time."[5] "This Negro play," wrote another reviewer, "celebrates with slow impressiveness a triumph of racial pride."[6]

How can a play be simultaneously specific and universal? This apparent paradox is easily resolved with the assertion that African-Americans are precisely as human—and African-American cultures just as universal or particular—as any other group. Hansberry herself pointed out the non-existence of the paradox:

Interviewer: The question, I'm sure, is asked you many times—you must be tired of it—someone comes up to you and says: "This is not really a Negro play; why, this could be about anybody! It's a play about people!" What is your reaction? What do you say?

Hansberry: Well[,] I hadn't noticed the contradiction because I'd always been under the impression that Negroes *are* people. . . . One of the most sound ideas in dramatic writing is that in order to create the universal, you must pay very great attention to the specific.[7]

Hansberry's solution to the apparent paradox did not go unnoticed or unremarked. Novelist John Oliver Killens, for example, wrote,

> Lorraine believed that . . . the literary road to universality is through local identity. Many critics said of *Raisin* that it is "universal," that it isn't specifically about Blacks. "It is about people. It could be about anybody." But a play that could be about anybody would most probably be about nobody at all. Lorraine was very clear on this point [in the above-quoted interview].[8]

Historian and editor Lerone Bennett, Jr found precisely the same solution to the apparent paradox:

> From my reading of Lorraine Hansberry, I get the feeling that she struggled all her life with the whole question of "universality." And I interpret her as having struggled against *false* definitions of "universality." . . . To my way of thinking, an artist is most universal when he's discussing the concrete issues of his own culture. It's the task of the artist to take the concrete and make it universal. . . . She was universal in her particularity.[9]

The paradox, then, is that a paradox was perceived at all, or that it continued to be perceived after Hansberry (and later, Killens, Bennett, and others[10]) had publicly resolved it. Why did critics persistently categorize *Raisin* as universal *or* specifically black? Why, when critics noted the fact that the play successfully communicated both universal and particular concerns, did they remark on this fact as a paradox or contradiction? In other words, why was the appearance of a paradox created and maintained? . . .

The claim that the play's characters are universal "people" without specific ties to African-American culture appears simply racist ("This is a well-written play; white people can relate to it; therefore it cannot be a black play"). Conversely, the assertion that the play is *not* universal but exclusively specific to African-Americans—that is, that the characters exist outside the category of "human"—seems equally racist. Upon closer examination, however, it is possible to discern both racist and anti-racist impulses in each claim.

The "particularizing" assertion can be separated into several different strands. In the most racist form, critics in this mode refused to acknowledge any difference between Hansberry's characters and stereotyped images of blacks. A few months after the play opened, Lorraine Hansberry noted "some of the prior attitudes which were brought into the theatre from the world outside. For in the minds of many, [the character of] Walter remains, despite the play, despite performance, what American racial traditions *wish* him to be: an exotic."[11] If audiences went to the theatre to see "the simple, lovable, and glandular 'Negro,'"[12] they would find him, regardless of what actually occurred on stage. Hansberry wrote,

> My colleagues and I were reduced to mirth and tears by that gentleman writing his review of our play in a Connecticut paper who remarked of his pleasure at seeing how "our dusky brethren" could "come up with a song and hum their troubles away." It did not disturb the writer in the least that there is no such implication in the entire three acts. He did not need it in the play; he had it in his head.[13]

Such blatant racism is related to the more subtle "people's culture" approach Eric Lott attacked in *Love and Theft: Blackface Minstrelsy and the American Working Class*. Lott defined the "people's culture" position as one that views minstrelsy as a more-or-less accurate reflection or aspect of "authentic" Negro culture. Lott's attack on this approach's ahistoricity and inaccuracy might seem not to apply to *Raisin*, which was obviously and deliberately locatable in black culture. However, the "people's culture" stance resembled that of some of the reviewers in that both approaches sought—or demanded— access to "authentic" black culture, as evidenced in critics' repeated praising of *Raisin* as "honest drama" with "vigor as well as veracity."[14] In other words, the "people's culture" approach and that of some of *Raisin*'s critics shared a common *impulse to access* perceived authentic black culture. And in doing so, they re-asserted whiteness as the norm.

The play's ability to appear to encapsulate "Negro experience" in the readily knowable, digestible, and non-threatening form of theatrical realism arguably satisfied this impulse and thus constituted the primary reason for the play's success among white audiences. In other words, the play's realism satisfied its white viewers in much the same way that minstrelsy satisfied its viewers by providing them with easy access to consumable perceived "Negro culture." *A Raisin in the Sun*, then, by making black experiences appear understandable to and consumable by white audiences, simultaneously made those experiences *collectable*. The bourgeois white viewer could display his or her new-found knowledge much as one might display a collection of "primitive" art; as James Clifford argues, "cultural description [can be] presented as a form of collecting."[15]

Collecting is a performance of power. To collect is to construct, limit, contain, display, and define. As Clifford observed, collections (even nonmaterial ones such as collected experiences of theatregoing) are necessarily organized taxonomically and hierarchically; thus collectors assert power over their possessions (which serve as metonyms for cultures).[16] The impulse for the white theatregoer to collect knowledge of "authentic" black experiences—through minstrelsy or *Raisin*'s realism—is therefore an impulse to perform (and thus actualize) white power.

Collecting is closely related to conservation, another performance of power to which Clifford devoted some attention: "Collecting—at least in the West, where time is generally thought to be linear and irreversible—implies a rescue of phenomena from inevitable historical decay or loss."[17] Clifford described the collecting of "primitive" visual art and the anthropological collecting of nonmaterial knowledge as similarly conservative projects: "Both discourses assume a primitive world in need of preservation, redemption, and representation."[18] White audiences' nonmaterial collecting of minority experiences through theatre attendance, then, could involve a similar conservative impulse. And as Clifford's colleague Donna Haraway noted, conservation is always intertwined with subjugation: "Once domination is complete, conservation is urgent."[19]

Finally, the assertion that *A Raisin in the Sun* was specifically and exclusively black effectively erased from the play Hansberry's class analysis. Many African-American critics and scholars have noticed and commented on this aspect of the play, but almost no white commentators have. Hansberry complained,

> Some writers have been astonishingly incapable of discussing [the character of Walter's] purely *class* aspirations and have persistently confounded them with what they consider to be an exotic being's longing to "wheel and deal" in what they consider to be (and what Walter never can) "the white man's world."[20]

The erasure of Hansberry's class analysis suggests white critics' unwillingness to engage with a black writer's intellect. In other words, white audiences who came to the theatre to see (and collect the experiences of) the "simple, lovable, and glandular 'Negro'"[21] (and encountering, to their disappointment, non-stereotyped characters[22]) could have preserved their mission by willfully ignoring anything that did not contribute to that project. Even the FBI, which investigated Lorraine Hansberry as a possible "danger to the Republic," labeled the play "not propagandistic."[23] This description, regarded as flattering by the FBI, revealed an unwillingness to engage with—or even recognize—the politics of the play.

By ignoring Hansberry's politics and recognizing only the play's specificity to black culture, white critics erased Hansberry's authority to speak about anything but herself. This action positioned blacks as if in a fishbowl: they could look at each other, but not at anything beyond their immediate context. This fishbowl could sit comfortably, decoratively, on a shelf in a white household; white people could peer through the glass (which contained and controlled the exotics and simultaneously kept the white spectator safely separated from the creatures) and enjoy their collection. In other words, erasing Hansberry's authority to speak about anything but her (white-defined) culture created a "glass" barrier which separated white audiences from the play's black creators and characters and rendered the subaltern collectable—and thus produced white power.

Furthermore, this "fishbowl" dynamic created a unidirectional gaze; that is to say, it positioned blacks as the object of both blacks' and whites' gazes, and simultaneously positioned whites as the empowered, invisible inspector. This action reified blacks' lives and experiences as collectable and simultaneously precluded the possibility of blacks inverting the dynamic and collecting (and thus disempowering) whites and their experiences. The fish cannot collect the human outside the bowl.

The interpretation of *Raisin* as specifically black (and distinctly not universal), however, also had non-racist, or even anti-racist aspects, most of which originated from African-American writers.

Hansberry wrote the play in response to a racist performance:

One night, after seeing a play I won't mention, I suddenly became disgusted with a whole body of material about Negroes. Cardboard characters. Cute dialect bits. Or hip-swinging musicals from exotic sources.[24]

The critic from Connecticut, then, was not entirely wrong when he read racist stereotypes into Hansberry's play: these stereotypes were diegetically present.

Black audiences apparently also read the play in the context of racist stereotypes. According to James Baldwin, the play drew unprecedented numbers of African-Americans to the theatre because "never before in American theater history had so much of the truth of black people's lives been seen on stage."[25] Overlap occurred, then, between the racist impulse to collect black experiences and the anti-racist impulse to see one's own experience reflected on stage (and to see stereotypes extirpated): both impulses hinged on the highly suspect notion of authenticity. The fact that two opposing impulses could exist in the same space contributed to the appearance of a paradox.

The play itself emphasized particularity within particularity through the character of Joseph Asagai, a Nigerian. According to Alex Haley, Hansberry achieved two goals through the character of Asagai. First, she

> helped to dispel the myth of the 'cannibal' with a bone in his hair. Her educated African character . . . was certainly the first time a large audience had seen and heard an African portrayed as carrying himself with dignity and being, moreover, a primary spokesman for sanity and progress. It must also have been the first time a mass audience had ever seen a black woman gracefully don African robes or wear an 'afro' hairstyle.[26]

Asagai, then, continued Hansberry's project of creating individual, specifically black characters who testified against stereotypes. Second, as Haley noted, *A Raisin in the Sun* was the first artistic work to popularize (on a large scale) the concept of a relationship between African-Americans and Africans.[27] By teasing out this relationship that specifically separated African-Americans from all other Americans, Hansberry again employed the particularizing approach—but to anti-racist ends.

As several critics—and Hansberry herself—have noted, however, Hansberry's particularism funneled into her universalism. Margaret B. Wilkerson posited that Hansberry's simultaneous particularism and universalism enabled *Raisin* to function as a bridge:

> Hansberry . . . [insists] upon a thorough probing of the individual within the specifics of culture, ethnicity and gender. In the midst of her expansiveness, she refuses to diminish the pain, suffering or truths of any one group

in order to benefit another, a factor which makes her plays particularly rich and her characters thoroughly complex. Hence, she can write authentically about a black family in *A Raisin in the Sun* and yet produce, in the same instance, a play which appeals to both Blacks and whites, bridging for a moment the historical and cultural gaps between them.

Her universalism, which redefines that much abused term, grows out of a deep, complex encounter with the specific terms of human experience as it occurs for Blacks, women, whites and many other groups of people. Her universalism is not facile, nor does it gloss over the things that divide people. She engages those issues, works through them, to find whatever may be, a priori, the human commonality that lies beneath.[28]

Obviously, there was an anti-racist project inherent to the demand that white audiences see themselves (i.e., the "universal") in black characters. And audiences responded to this demand: scholars such as Lerone Bennett, Jr. have commented on the "curious identification some elements of the non-black community felt toward the play."[29] However, within this dynamic—which Hansberry deliberately created from an antiracist politic—racist interpretations abounded.

The universalist interpretation of the play was used to deny and erase the particularity on which Hansberry insisted. In this way, universalism functioned much like the collecting instinct of the "people's culture" approach: the latter sought black culture in order to acquire and preserve it and thus assert power over it; the former denied and erased black culture in order to control and assert power over it. Once again, opposing projects overlapped and contributed to the appearance of a paradox. . . .

Lerone Bennett, Jr. was correct when he called Hansberry "a kind of herald, a person announcing the coming of something," as when he described a nameless something "in the air . . . and whites felt it as well as Blacks."[41] Perhaps that subconsciously anticipated "something"—so feared by the creators and maintainers of the paradox—was a postmodern, globalized culture in which boundaries between universal and particular, white and nonwhite, collector and collected, are unstable. A world in which the subaltern speaks back; in which culture flows not only from the "top, down," but in all chaotic directions; a world, in the words of Arjun Appadurai, in which "the United States [and by extension, whiteness] is no longer the puppeteer of a world system of images, but is only one node of a complex transnational construction of imaginary landscapes."[42] Through the desperate creation and maintenance of the appearance of the paradox—which in turn created and maintained a static boundary between universal and particular, white and black—white people created the illusion that they could collect minority experiences without being collected themselves.

Notes

1. George Murray, "'Raisin in Sun' Terrific Theater," *Chicago American*, 27 Feb. 1959, 19.

2. Sydney J. Harris, "Sydney Harris Reviews: 'A Raisin in the Sun,'" *Chicago Daily News*, 11 Feb. 1959, 39.

3. George Oppenheimer, "On Stage," newspaper unknown, 25 March 1959, in file, *"A Raisin in the Sun*: Clippings," New York Public Library for the Performing Arts, Billy Rose Collection.

4. Claudia Cassidy, "On the Aisle: Warm Heart, Backbone, Funnybone in Blackstone Play and Cast," *Chicago Daily Tribune*, 12 February 1959, F1.

5. Brooks Atkinson, "A Raisin in the Sun," in *On Stage: Selected Theater Reviews from The New York Times, 1920–1970*, eds. Bernard Beckerman and Howard Siegman (New York: Arno Press, 1970), 402.

6. "A Simple Story: Triumph of Negro Pride," *London Times*, 5 Aug. 1959, n.p., in file, *"A Raisin in the Sun*: Clippings," New York Public Library for the Performing Arts, Billy Rose Collection.

7. Lorraine Hansberry [assembled and edited by Robert Nemiroff], *To Be Young, Gifted, and Black* (New York: New American Library, Inc., 1970), 128.

8. John Oliver Killens, "Lorraine Hansberry: On Time!" *Freedomways: A Quarterly Review of the Freedom Movement* 19 (1979): 275.

9. Lerone Bennett, Jr. and Margaret G. Burroughs, "A Lorraine Hansberry Rap," *Freedomways: A Quarterly Review of the Freedom Movement* 19 (1979): 232.

10. I have chosen not to attempt to create any chronology of criticism. In other words, I have not traced the ways in which the

play's critical reception changed over time, nor have I foregrounded time as an important factor in this study. My purpose in this paper is not to write a history of the play's critical reception, but rather to unpack the ideas that have swirled around the play from 1959 until today. Also because I am not foregrounding any chronology, I use the words "African-American" and "black" interchangeably when I refer to people of a nonspecified time; I use "Negro" only when I refer specifically to blacks prior to the early 1960s.

11. Lorraine Hansberry, "Willie Loman, Walter Younger, and He Who Must Live," *The Village Voice*, 12 August 1959, 7, 8. Emphasis in original. In this article, the word "racial" was mispublished as "radical"; however, on August 19, the *Voice* corrected it to "racial." I have corrected the quote for ease in reading.

12. Ibid., 8.

13. Ibid.

14. Frank Ashton and Brooks Atkinson, respectively, quoted in Lorraine Hansberry, *A Raisin in the Sun*, New York: The New American Library, 1966, back cover.

15. James Clifford, *The Predicament of Culture: Twentieth-Century Ethnography, Literature, and Art* (Cambridge, MA: Harvard University Press, 1988): 215.

16. Ibid., 218.

17. Clifford, 231.

18. Ibid., 200.

19. Donna Haraway, *Primate Visions: Gender, Race, and Nature in the World of Modern Science* (New York: Routledge, 1989): 34.

20. Hansberry, "Willie Loman," 8; emphasis in original.

21. Hansberry, "Willie Loman," 8.

22. The assertion that the characters are not stereotyped is not without controversy. Many critics, both black and white, have noted that the play "abounds with types: Mama is a tyrannical but good-natured matriarch; Walter, a frustrated young man surrounded by too many women; Beneatha, a free-thinking college student; the African Asagai, a poetic revolutionary; and the one white man, a cliché-ridden suburbanite" (Abramson, 254). In particular, the character of Mama was "charged by critics" with being "a reactionary black 'mammy'" (Adrienne Rich, "The Problem with Lorraine Hansberry," *Freedomways: A Quarterly Review of the Freedom Movement* 19 [1979]: 252)—a characterization vociferously contradicted by black writers such as Amiri Baraka and Margaret B. Wilkerson (Amiri Baraka, "'Raisin in the Sun's' Enduring Passion," *The Washington Post*, 16 November 1986, n.p, in file, "*A Raisin in the Sun*: Clippings," New York Public Library for the Performing Arts, Billy Rose Collection; Wilkerson, "Anniversary," 122, 125, 128). The point is not that the play was necessarily devoid of stereotypes, but rather that any

stereotypes it may have contained were certainly far less pronounced and racist than those of minstrelsy.

23. Margaret B. Wilkerson, "*A Raisin in the Sun*: Anniversary of an American Classic," in *Performing Feminisms: Feminist Critical Theory and Theatre*, ed. Sue-Ellen Case (Baltimore, MD: Johns Hopkins University Press, 1990), 122.

24. Lorraine Hansberry, quoted in Nan Robertson, "Dramatist Against Odds," *New York Times*, 8 March 1959 (In file, "A Raisin in the Sun," New York Public Library, Schomburg Collection); quoted in Doris E. Abramson, *Negro Playwrights in the American Theatre, 1925–1959*, New York: Columbia University Press, 1967, 240.

25. Elizabeth Brown-Guillory, *Their Place on the Stage: Black Women Playwrights in America* (Westport, CT: Greenwood Press, 1988): 34.

26. Alex Haley, "The Once and Future Vision of Lorraine Hansberry," *Freedomways: A Quarterly Review of the Freedom Movement* 19 (1979): 279.

27. Ibid, 278–9.

28. Margaret B. Wilkerson, "Lorraine Hansberry: The Complete Feminist," *Freedomways: A Quarterly Review of the Freedom Movement* 19 (1979): 237.

29. Bennett and Burroughs, 230.

41. Bennett and Burroughs, 229.

42. Arjun Appadurai, "Disjuncture and Difference in the Global Cultural Economy," in *The Phantom Public Sphere*, ed. Bruce Robbins (Minneapolis, MN: Minnesota University Press, 1993): 273.

PHILIP UKO EFFIONG ON THE PLAY'S AFRICAN ALLUSIONS

It is also through Mama that the equivalent of African ancestral reverence is portrayed. After Walter has been duped of part of the family's insurance money, Mama ponders over visions she has had of her late husband:

> I seen . . . him . . . night after night . . . come in . . . and look at the rug . . . and then look at me . . . the red showing in his eyes . . . the veins moving in his head . . . I seen him grow thin and old before he was forty . . . working and working and working like somebody's old horse . . . killing himself . . . and you—give it all away in a day— (II.iii.129)

Mama's contemplation matches common African beliefs in a cyclical life and death worldview where ancestral spirits exist as reinvigorated cosmic forces demanding obeisance and remembrance. That the patriarch here has toiled to guarantee self and posthumous survival demonstrates the important point that ancestral and elderly veneration has to be earned. Delineating archetypal ancestral roles, the patriarchal spirit here is invoked to inspire hope and perseverance.

A more direct reference to Africa is reached through the Nigerian character Asagai, who represents "the first appearance in black American drama of an African intellectual as a major character" (Ro 1985, 567). He is racially proud, handsome, and progressive, an intellectual and political activist whom Mama describes as "a pretty thing" (I.ii.65). Asagai is Hansberry's medium for demonstrating a periodic nostalgia for Africa, even if it is more mental than real. Comparable with concepts like double consciousness and cultural denial, the nostalgic feeling has been summarized by Lloyd Brown as the "Black American's duality" (1974, "Ironist," 241). In essence, Asagai embodies part of "a very narrow escape hatch" which Margaret Wilkerson sees as a channel out of the "abrasive contraries" in which the Youngers are submerged (1986, "Anniversary," 442).

As modern African activist, Asagai is a revolutionary model for Beneatha, Walter, and Black America. Operating in an African-American setting, he strengthens, but does not resolve, the destabilized ancestral connection between Africans and Black Americans. In his relationship with Beneatha, he becomes a metaphoric member of the Younger family. Just as the Youngers are cynical about their future in a White neighborhood, Asagai is also unsure of his fate among his own people whom he plans to finally return to with new political doctrines.

For the emasculated Walter and identity-seeking Beneatha, Asagai also serves as social model. He signifies the archetypal supremacy of culture and spirituality over material profit. His repudiation of Walter's blind fixation to materialism corroborates his possession of the type of dignity the latter lacks. Walter's loss of money does not upset Asagai's "belief in the transcendent power of man and woman" (Wilkerson 1986, "Anniversary," 451). Instead he warns Beneatha against using her brother's error as an excuse to give up on "the ailing human race," since one mistake is not enough reason to bring a movement to an end (III.135). Asagai understands that he must armor himself with the same type of faith when he returns to his own country to fight poverty, ignorance, and foreign rule.

Beneatha apprentices herself to Asagai in order to learn more about her roots, and creates illusions of becoming "a queen of the Nile!" (I.ii.66). This way, Asagai is able to evolve into a cultural conduit, informing Beneatha about African history, belief systems, practices, and ongoing battles against imperialism. Her cultural awareness is broadened by his instructions on African clothing, music, song, and dance, and by his gifts of a Nigerian name, *Alaiyo*, and a Nigerian robe. Her robe and natural "afro" hair presage the new wave of fashion and hairstyles that were embraced by Black Americans in the 1960s.

African names are well known for their philosophical meanings and messages. The West African (Yoruba)[2] name, *Alaiyo*, translates into "One for Whom Bread—Food—Is Not Enough," and suggests a yearning or emotional hunger for *more* (I.ii.65). Within the context of *A Raisin*, *Alaiyo* stresses the hunger and thirst by marginalized peoples, in this case Blacks, for the contentment that liberty alone can provide. It is satisfaction that cannot be obtained from ordinary food.

Beneatha's personal odyssey toward cultural rebirth is crowned in her version of an African folk dance that she performs with Walter, and in her Nigerian robe. It is a Yoruba "dance of welcome" performed by women when the "men (return) to the village" (II.i.77). The dance is both magical and therapeutic, for she draws Walter into it and reaches out briefly to a brother whom she despises. Brother and sister dance to the rhythm of a Yoruba song, briefly welcoming and engaging in a segment of their heritage, though it is a small segment. The performance follows a repetitive pattern with Walter imagining himself as "a great chief, a descendant of Chaka" fighting alongside Jomo Kenyatta (II.i.78). He chants short warring declarations laced with floral and faunal symbols, to which Beneatha responds "OWIMOWEH" or "OCOMOGOSIAY." The entire process is structured on the call and response arrangement common in African folklore from various parts of the continent (II.i.76–79). Transformed at the end of the dance, Walter's drunken, yet eloquent, exhortation reaches out to Blacks beyond his family, linking African-American struggles to a global Black saga. He calls on "MY BLACK BROTHERS! . . . to prepare for the GREATNESS OF THE TIME!" (II.i.79).

The entire song and dance scenario is actually stereotypical to some degree, and yet it invokes racial pride and dignity, not savagery. Beneatha and Walter delve into their souls and succeed for one brief moment to mine strength from their ethnic past in idealized fashion. In identifying with African warriors and heroes, their dance has the potential to incite both characters on to conquer familial and societal pressures and conflicts. But the potential does not necessarily substantiate the extent to which they are energized and provoked by the cultural experience, especially since Walter and Beneatha's *Yoruba* dance turns out to be more fantasy than reality. Their reactions are ambiguous, though sincere, and play out the truth that Black Americans recapture their history largely from the standpoint of the Western culture in which they exist. While Africa offers a vital historical and cultural frame of reference, it remains a distant land largely unknown and often illusory. Walter's drunken state during the sub drama only reinforces this dilemma. His condition does not immediately demean the historical relevance of Africa or the self-discovery he engages in, but it demystifies the sanctity of the event and shifts it further from reality to illusion. The result is an aura of triviality that is compounded when, shortly after, Walter is humbled by the realization that his actions are silly, not culturally inspiring. His final reactions to cultural nationalism are ambivalent and raise the unpopular possibility that Africa, after all, may not be all glorious or highly desired.

Walter's vague reclamation of Africa prepares the reader/audience for the entry of George Murchison, the African-American who, at the other extreme, spurns Africa. He is the direct opposite of Asagai and Beneatha, and personifies, in some ways, those conventional, uninformed facts about Africa that are still largely predictable. The classic victim of cultural rape featured in a lot of African-American writing, Beneatha describes him as an "assimilationist Negro," who "give(s) up his own culture and submerge(s) himself completely in the dominant . . . oppressive culture!" (II.i.81) In an argument with her, Murchison says, "Let's face it, baby, your heritage is nothing but a bunch of raggedy-assed spirituals and some grass huts!" (II.i.81). In response, Beneatha immediately dispels his parochial ideas with bold claims that may require verification: "You are standing there in your splendid ignorance talking about people who were the first to smelt iron on the face of the earth! The Ashanti were performing surgical operations when the English were still tattooing themselves with blue dragons!" (Il.i.81)

But Beneatha's first defense of Africa actually takes place in an earlier scene involving she and Mama. Although Mama's ignorance of Africa does not imply the type of flagrant disregard expressed by Murchison, her derogatory remarks about the continent are derisive enough for Beneatha to reeducate her. Here, Beneatha's strategy is to convince Mama that a prejudicial sentiment underlines most distorted opinions on the region. When she tells Mama that "all anyone seems to know when it comes to Africa is Tarzan," she is criticizing the concept of Africa being helpless and regressive only until it is rescued by European intrusion (I.ii.57). John Henrik Clarke makes a similar point when he warns that misinformed African images have been used to justify the "rape, pillage and destruction of African cultural patterns" by Europe (11). Because she is of the same view, Beneatha informs Mama that her (Mama's) financial support for missionary work in Africa neglects the real problem: the forced intervention by "the British and French" (I.ii.57). Part of the excuse for European imperialism, after all, centers on the need to civilize and convert African pagans, and shifts focus from the criminal, the colonizer. Hansberry deliberately sets out to subvert common erroneous beliefs about Africa, and uses Beneatha as her mouthpiece. She does succeed to a large extent and Brown-Guillory commends her for "[revolutionizing] the way Americans, blacks and whites, perceived Africans" (1988, 35). And yet it is not Hansberry's prime goal to simply depict Africa as rich and majestic.

Irrespective of how laudable some of the images of Africa are in *A Raisin*, Hansberry does not romanticize the yearning for a culturally rich, spiritual homeland. Africa also surfaces as a background afflicted by political weaknesses that have existed for generations, many of which continue to exist. Asagai in some ways exemplifies both culture-contact and African independent struggles that are referred to in a largely practical manner. But there are also skeptical hints at possible flaws within independent Africa. When Asagai envisages a progressive autonomous Africa, Beneatha's reaction is cynical and she, on the other hand, predicts the future emergence of neo-colonial African regimes. "Independence and then what?" she asks. "What about all the crooks and thieves and just plain idiots who will come into power and steal and plunder as before—only now they will be black ... WHAT ABOUT THEM?!" (III.133–34) Years later, Beneatha (Hansberry) was proven right. Africa has had more than its fair share of dictatorial regimes apparent in the bloody administrations of Idi Amin, the deposed president of Uganda; Jean-Bédel Bokassa, the overthrown, now deceased leader of the impoverished Central African Republic; Mobutu Sese Sekou, the former president, now deceased, of Zaire; Samuel Doe of Liberia, killed in a 1990 uprising against his government; and Sani Abacha of Nigeria who died under mysterious circumstances in 1998. Self-rule in Africa still relies on European political systems, which remains an unresolved controversy. Hansberry rejects a historical perspective depicting Africa as an entity with impeccable viable systems, one that fails to address immanent political realities.

Despite his self-esteem and heroic status, even Asagai is not the infallible, distinguished African. In his relationship with Beneatha, he makes typical male chauvinistic and female objectifying comments when he tells her that "between a man and a woman there need be only one kind of feeling" and "for a woman it should be enough" (I.ii.62–63). Beneatha responds "with feminine vengeance" and assures Asagai that "I know—because that's what it says in all the novels men write. But it isn't. Go ahead and laugh—but I'm not interested in being someone's little episode in America" (I.ii.63).

But compared to the inclusion of African themes and characters in early 20th century, 1930s, and 1940s musicals; and in some 1920s dramas like Willis Richardson's *The Black Horseman* (1929), Edward J. Mcoo's *Ethiopia at the Bar* (1924), and Maud Cuney-Hare's *Antar of Araby* (1929), Hansberry's Asagai introduces a relatively new insight on Africa. The above musicals and plays "lent themselves to romantic feelings about unparticularized African characters" (Hatch 1980, "African Influences," 18). Hansberry, on the other hand, creates a particularized African in Asagai who she uses to dissipate the myth that Africa does not accept its descendants in America. This acceptance is confirmed, tentatively though, when Asagai invites Beneatha to Nigeria: "Nigeria. Home. I will . . . teach you the old songs and ways of our people—and, in time, we will pretend that you have only been away for a day" (Il.iii.116). But Beneatha asks for time to consider Asagai's proposal. Her hesitation suggests that she might not be very eager to go "home" to Nigeria after all. Earlier on, after, she flaunts her Nigerian robes with pride, she changes into something else for her date with Murchison (II.i.85). In spite of what seems to be a strong longing for African values, Beneatha, like many African-Americans, is limited by how deeply she can, and, perhaps, wants to accept and relate to Africa. Her real home is America after all. Africa is historically and culturally invaluable, but it can also be mythic, illusive, and inaccessible. This apparent inability, sometimes reluctance, to "reach" Africa in spite of "nostalgia" for the land, illustrates another angle in DuBois' double consciousness philosophy. Hansberry refuses to back away from this truth and finally explores themes that address Africa without generalizing or advancing utopian perspectives.

Because Hansberry studied African history extensively, she does not simply idealize the continent or concentrate subjectively on its strengths and exploitation by European imperialism. It is for this reason, too, that she recognizes certain weaknesses within modern Africa, one being a fast growing neo-colonial class as portrayed by Asagai in *A Raisin* and Abioseh in *Les Blancs.*

Notes
2. The Yoruba ethnic group is the second largest in Nigeria and occupies the western part of the country. Yoruba people can also be found in the West African countries of Togo, Benin Republic, and Dahomey.

TRUDIER HARRIS ON PORTRAYALS OF STRONG BLACK WOMEN

It is no coincidence that the physically large Claudia McNeil was selected to play the role of Mama Lena Younger on the stage as well as in the 1961 Columbia Pictures film version of the play, for the mimetic quality extended from subject matter and characterization to cast selection.[16] Hansberry's description of Mama Lena probably influenced the selection of McNeil as well:

> MAMA *enters. She is a woman in her early sixties, full-bodied and* strong. *She is one of those women of a certain grace and beauty who wear it so unobtrusively that it takes a while to notice. Her dark-brown face is surrounded by the total whiteness of her hair, and being a woman who has adjusted to many things in life and overcome many more, her face is full of strength.*[17]

Throughout the play, Mama Lena's size and physical strength are focal points for action. On stage, Mama Lena towered over the women cast as Ruth and Beneatha; photographs from those productions make the contrasts strikingly obvious. In reading the play, her sheer force of will is apparent in contrast to everyone around her as it looms larger and carries more force. Body size and strength of character simultaneously operate to locate Mama Lena in the stereotype of the domineering strong black woman character as well as to lift her slightly out of it because she is literally the prototype for what later would be judged to be stereotypical.

This size factor is especially important in the scene that sets Mama Lena's biological tyranny in bas relief, that is, in the scene in which she slaps Beneatha for denying the existence of God. When Beneatha ends a tirade with "There simply is no blasted God—there is only man and it is he who makes miracles!," "(MAMA *absorbs this speech, studies her daughter and rises slowly and crosses to* BENEATHA *and slaps her powerfully across the face. After, there is only silence and the daughter drops her eyes from her mother's face, and* MAMA *is very tall before her)*" (39). Mama Lena combines physical size with moral strength when she forces Beneatha to repeat after her: "Now—you say after me, in my mother's house there is still God" (39). The reluctant Beneatha repeats the phrase in spite of her unwillingness to do so. And although Mama is *"too disturbed for triumphant posture"* as she leaves the scene, she has nonetheless made her point about where power resides in the family and who shapes reality. But she is not too disturbed to say as she departs: "There are some ideas we ain't going to have in this house. Not long as I am at the head of this family," and Beneatha meekly replies, "Yes, ma'am" (39). Mama Lena's way of looking at the universe is reinstated, verbally and physically if not substantively, and, in this setting, the physical forcing of verbal acquiescence seems to carry the day. As J. Charles Washington points out, Mama Lena's "actions rarely receive censure even though they are far less than ideal."[18] As African American scholar Sally Ann Ferguson asserts, the violence Mama Lena exhibits is an acceptable dimension of the woman in this tradition who is in charge of her household.[19] Ruth adds her brick to the wall of the status quo by asserting to Mama Lena after Beneatha's departure: "You just got strong-willed children and it takes a strong woman like you to keep 'em in hand" (40), a comment that encompasses the physical and the moral.

Mama's logic in reaction to Beneatha's blasphemy is centered upon the belief that no child borne of her body could have strayed so far from the moral values of its mother, a concept tied to the biblical notion that like trees bear like fruit ("By their fruits ye shall know them"). Beneatha therefore cannot remain unrecognizable because she has come from a recognizable source, thus Mama Lena presumably slaps her back into that familiar recognition. It is the "Mama" position that has given Mama Lena the "right" to slap Beneatha, thereby making name, size, biology, and morality equal parts of the authority she wields."[20] Beneatha might assert after Mama Lena leaves the scene, "I see also that everybody thinks it's all right for Mama to be a tyrant. But all the tyranny in the world will never put a God in the heavens!" (40), but *in Mama Lena's presence*, Beneatha does as she is told.[21] Neither she nor Walter has the will to stand toe-to-toe, so to speak, with Mama, state a case, and win an argument. Mama's physical and moral power *as mother* are not to be challenged. She usually gets little resistance when she insists upon imposing her view of reality upon her family.

Mama Lena is like a hurricane that carves its path through any obstacles it encounters. That force, guided by the same attributes that determine her behavior with Beneatha, enables her to direct the lives of Travis, Ruth, and Walter Lee. Consider the scene in which Mama Lena questions Ruth about how she has prepared Travis' breakfast:

MAMA . . . What you fix for his breakfast this morning?
RUTH (*Angrily*) I feed my son, Lena!
MAMA I ain't meddling—(*Underbreath; busy-bodyish*) I just noticed all last week he had cold cereal, and when it starts getting this chilly in the fall a child ought to have some hot grits or something when he goes out in the cold—
RUTH (*Furious*) I gave him hot oats—is that all right!
MAMA I ain't meddling. (*Pause*) Put a lot of nice butter on it? (RUTH *shoots her an angry look and does not reply*) He likes lots of butter.
RUTH (*Exasperated*) Lena— (28–29)

At this point, Mama Lena simply turns the discussion to focus on Beneatha and the conversation she has been having with

Walter Lee. That Ruth makes the transition with her is further indication that Ruth does not have the desire or the force of will to try to stand against Mama Lena overly long; besides, Mama Lena has made her point and, by reincorporating Ruth into a congenial conversation, she exhibits her power to disrupt as well as to soothe. In discussing Travis, Mama Lena not only ignores Ruth's anger and exasperation, but she makes it clear through her tone and persistence that no obstacle will prevent her from reaching her ultimate objective: confirmation that Travis has been fed in a way that Mama Lena would approve. It is not a conversation that Ruth will forget, and whether or not Ruth appreciates it, the conversation will influence the future meals she prepares for her son. By attempting to usurp Ruth's authority as Travis' mother, Mama Lena indicates that that relationship is merely nominal; the true "Mama" is Mama Lena.[22] She recognizes no boundary of presumed motherly authority in connection to Ruth that would prevent her from questioning Ruth, and she refuses to desist because Ruth is angry, offended, embarrassed, or otherwise made uncomfortable because Mama Lena is questioning her parenting abilities. She at least shapes her inquiries in the form of questions; more often than not, she speaks in the imperative voice.[23] Nonetheless, "the Mama"'s agenda supersedes everyone else's. The impact upon Ruth is apparent in her halting behavior throughout the play as well as in her relationship to Walter Lee; she is basically mousy, acquiescent. She can never claim a space as the primary woman in this household and is thereby pushed into a peripheral, ghostlike position. Ruth may also be referred to as "Mama," but her positional relationship in the family diminishes the use of that word in comparison to Mama Lena's power and position. Mama Lena's strength as mother and "wife" to Walter Lee and as "mother" to Travis nearly makes Ruth superfluous.

It is important as well to highlight again the physical space in which these exchanges occur and to note its possible impact upon these interactions. This is Mama Lena's space, *her house*. Ruth is therefore as much a guest as she is a daughter- or sister-in-law. This near outsider status and the knowledge that her husband, after the wedding ceremony, has simply taken her home to his mother's space may contribute its share to Ruth's character. Ruth has undoubtedly witnessed many scenes in which status by reason of space figures into the argument. Mama Lena uses ownership of this space on several occasions as the basis for demanding certain actions or acquiescence to her beliefs.

Mama Lena's biological tyranny and moral self-righteousness are keenly apparent in scenes in which Mama Lena directs the relationship between Walter Lee and Ruth. The first occurs when Mama Lena demands that Walter Lee talk with Ruth about her planned abortion, which is unfortunately just at the moment the long-awaited insurance check arrives:

> MAMA Son—I think you ought to talk to your wife . . . I'll go on out and leave you alone if you want—
> WALTER I can talk to her later—Mama, look—
> MAMA Son—
> WALTER WILL SOMEBODY PLEASE LISTEN TO ME TODAY!
> MAMA (*Quietly*) I don't 'low no yellin' in this house, Walter Lee, and you know it— (WALTER *stares at them in frustration and starts to speak several times*) And there ain't going to be no investing in no liquor stores. I don't aim to have to speak on that again. . . .
> WALTER I'm going out! . . .
> MAMA (*Still quietly*) Walter Lee— (*She waits and he finally turns and looks at her*) Sit down.
> WALTER I'm a grown man, Mama.
> MAMA Ain't nobody said you wasn't grown. But you still in my house and my presence. And as long as you are— you'll talk to your wife civil. Now sit down. . . . [Walter Lee later jumps up] I said sit there now, I'm talking to you! (57–59)[24]

As many critics have pointed out, Mama Lena essentially treats Walter Lee like a little boy. He is being called into accountability as an adolescent might be who has just thrown a baseball through a window. What makes the scene so compelling in the strength scenario is the incongruity between the substance of the calling into accountability and the form it takes. Abortion is not a subject one would expect small children to be summoned to discuss, yet the summoning here is precisely in that seemingly innocent form. Mama Lena's control of her children's lives enables the summoning, and her moral superiority enables her to broach a subject that in this environment is usually not broachable.

This scene perhaps highlights Mama Lena's commanding presence more than any other in the play. However, as this sequence plays itself out, she gets less than she desires. She fully expects that Walter Lee, like Big Walter and like Mama Lena herself, will "do the right thing":

> MAMA Son—do you know your wife is expecting another baby? . . . I think Ruth is thinking 'bout getting rid of that child.
>
> WALTER (*Slowly understanding*) No—no—Ruth wouldn't do that. . . .
>
> RUTH (*Beaten*) Yes I would too, Walter. (*Pause*) I gave her a five-dollar down payment.
>
> (*There is total silence as the man stares at his wife and the mother stares at her son*)
>
> MAMA (*Presently*) Well— (*Tightly*) Well—son, I'm waiting to hear you say something . . . I'm waiting to hear how you be your father's son. Be the man he was . . . (*Pause*) Your wife say she going to destroy your child. And I'm waiting to hear you talk like him and say we a people who give children life, not who destroys them— (*She rises*) I'm waiting to see you stand up and look like your daddy and say we done give up one baby to poverty and that we ain't going to give up nary another one . . . I'm waiting.
>
> WALTER Ruth—
>
> MAMA If you a son of mine, tell her! (WALTER *turns, looks at her and can say nothing. She continues, bitterly*) You . . . you are a disgrace to your father's memory. Somebody get me my hat. (61, 62)

The hurricane carves out its path; it does not pause to consider the house it topples or the tree it uproots. Family history and biology will not allow Mama Lena—at least not yet—to entertain the possibility that her actions might be detrimental to her son and her daughter-in-law. The position of "mama" enables her to violate privacy; indeed, the psychological violation of privacy is but the counterpart to the physical violation that ensues simply by virtue of the family's living quarters. Mama Lena's larger moral imperative does not grant to Ruth the power of alternative choices, for there can be no choice in Mama Lena's scheme except for her daughter-in-law to give birth to an unaffordable child, then love it—or pretend to—and raise it accordingly (and it is clear that Ruth would prefer not to go through with the abortion if she can help it). There is thus a simplicity inherent in Mama Lena's moral strength, a simple either/or formula that always figures right and wrong as clear-cut choices; there can be no gray areas. That simplicity adds another dimension to the strength formula; it makes control a clear-cut proposition just as it similarly makes reaction to control a simple and easy thing to do.

Anguish that Ruth may feel for having her burdening secret bluntly announced to her husband never figures in her or Mama Lena's actions, for Mama Lena's limited moral imperative denies the possibility of rejection of her righteous course of action. Embarrassment is not an allowable emotion in the strong black woman character's frame of reference. Hansberry seemingly gives Mama Lena the upper hand by not portraying overly much Ruth's reaction to the very drama that is intensely shaping her life. Certainly Ruth staggers and faints, but readers and viewers do not pause with concern about those occurrences for very long, for the larger issue is shaped by Mama Lena. Mama Lena can hold Ruth and soothe her in the staggering episode, but she has not created an environment in which Ruth could confide in her woman-to-woman and, indeed, their not being age peers might prevent that as well; she must therefore deduce that Ruth is pregnant. Once that knowledge is confirmed, Mama Lena can make it public, but she does not allow comparable public exposure of information about her. For example, when Walter Lee confronts her directly on the day she makes the down payment on the house, her response to his "Where did you go this afternoon?" and "What kind of business?" is "You know better than to question me like a child, Brother" (75, 76). Yet to Mama Lena, all the adults in her household are children. Ruth's pain, therefore, is Mama Lena's to manipulate as she wishes.[25]

Although Mama Lena seemingly "loses" in the scene in that Walter Lee does not avow his love for Ruth and his support for their unborn child, the traits that define her as the strong black woman character are nonetheless sharply apparent. Throughout, she directs—or attempts to direct—the action between husband and wife. She becomes marriage counselor, judge, and jury in addition to parent. Like Beneatha not being *allowed* to deny God, Walter Lee cannot possibly be *allowed* to deny the parental heritage bequeathed to him by Mama Lena and Big Walter. By pushing him toward identification with that, Mama Lena seeks again to reinstate the values most familiar to her. Again, the majority of the audience viewing the play in 1959 would have held similar attitudes toward abortion; therefore, this scene is especially compelling in the argument that would allow Mama Lena's point of view to prevail despite her domineering postures.

Yet there is a conflict here that Mama Lena obviously does not consider. She has raised her son Walter Lee, and although she now demands that he be a man, it is not apparent that she has previously allowed him to be so. Certainly he has observed the ostensible markers of manhood: marrying and fathering a child. But he has not assumed the responsibility of partnering that wife or raising that child, for Mama Lena has shouldered most of those responsibilities. Now a real crisis has arisen. It calls for action in keeping with Mama Lena's teachings but one that would assert an independence from her in Walter's desire to be a father in spite of the economic and family conditions. Walter is unable to respond. His lack of response, however, does not mean that the strong black woman character has been toppled from her position of family dominance. She has simply been temporarily thwarted from having her way in the lives of her children. After all, she ends the scene with a command: "Somebody get me my hat" (62), thereby still in control of many of the actions of those around her. . . .

However, she has one more low point to undergo with Walter Lee—the scene in which he plans to accept the money from Karl Lindner, the white man sent to buy out their interest in the house in all-white Clybourne Park. Mama Lena insists that Travis be on hand if Walter Lee is going to go through the minstrel act he has previewed for the family: "No. Travis, you stay right here [instead of going downstairs]. And you make him understand what you doing, Walter Lee. You teach him good. Like Willy Harris taught you. You show where our five generations done come to. Go ahead, son—" (126). With those admonitions (strongly and powerfully directive in spite of a presumably undermined Mama Lena), and with Travis' merry expectations, it is impossible for Walter Lee to play the role of the minstrel or to allow Lindner to buy his family's dignity. In the early stages of this scene, Hansberry emphasizes twice that Walter Lee is "*like a small boy*" (126, 127). It could be argued, then, that this small boy has lost his mother's approval and, in a scene that parallels the first scene of the play between Ruth and Travis, must work to be restored to her good graces. The "*small boy*" will finally—or seemingly so—be transformed into a man. When Walter Lee tells Lindner that the Youngers will move into his neighborhood, "(MAMA *has her eyes closed and is rocking back and forth as though she were in church, with her head nodding the amen yes)*" (128). The small boy has indeed won his mother's approval. . . .

When her family's actions are to her advantage and approval, Mama Lena slides into the role supportive of those actions. Lindner tries to appeal to her, only to be met with this comment from Mama: "I am afraid you don't understand. My son said we was going to move and there ain't nothing left for me to say. (*Shaking her head with double meaning*) You know how these young folks is nowadays, mister. Can't do a thing with 'em. Good-bye" (128). Since very little Walter Lee has said during the course of the play has been taken seriously (consider the breakfast scene with Ruth or his expressions of his dreams to Beneatha and Mama Lena), Mama Lena only supports his final position because it is in line with her own. And, no matter the nobility of Walter Lee's decision, perhaps Walter Lee has come to realize that making peace with Mama Lena is infinitely preferable to losing the respect of his entire family. Though Mama Lena claims to have lost her power of influence, it is clear immediately upon Lindner's departure that she is just as directive at the end of Act III as she was at the beginning of Act I: "Ruth, put Travis' good jacket on him . . . Walter Lee, fix your tie and tuck your shirt in, you look just like somebody's hoodlum" (128). The voice of power remains the voice of power, and the queen has not moved an inch from her throne. . . .

Mama Lena is in her 60s, and Hansberry writes that she is still a beautiful woman. In the current action of the play, however, she has no gentleman caller(s) and seems thoroughly devoted to the memory of Big Walter.[32] It is worthwhile to examine the legend of that relationship, for Mama Lena uses it in several instances to coerce her family to certain attitudes and actions. Though no mention of church going occurs in the current action of the play, Mama Lena comments, when she is confronted with Beneatha's blasphemy, that she and Big Walter took the children to Sunday School every Sunday; that memory is intended as a weapon to inspire Beneatha to toe the proper religious line. Mama Lena also uses Big Walter's example to inspire Walter Lee to accept his responsibility to Ruth and their unborn child, and memory of Big Walter's hard work provides the emotional depth of the betrayal when Walter Lee gives the money away. Yet what of the intimate relationship between Mama Lena and Big Walter? Has he been only a provider and concerned father? What of the privacy of their relationship? Certainly they had sex, but was there any romance there? Part of her heightened reaction to Ruth's contemplation of abortion is memory of the death of little Claude and how Big Walter responded to that tragedy. But that is precisely the area of concern in relation to her strength, for Mama Lena charts Big Walter's reaction to the death more so than her own, as if her strength has enabled her to endure the loss better than her husband—in spite of the child having issued from her very body.

More important, by making Big Walter larger than life, she diminishes his faults, and it is in those faults that we gauge what she has given up—or been forced to endure—in their relationship. She says: "Crazy 'bout his children! God knows there was plenty wrong with Walter Younger—hard-headed, mean, kind of wild with women—plenty wrong with him. But he sure loved his children. Always wanted them to have something—be something" (33). Mama Lena's intimate relationship with her husband is buried in the set aside phrase where she names his faults. What did his "hard-headedness" mean for her as his wife? How did his "meanness" affect her and indeed their children? And is "kind of wild with women" another one of those toning down expressions to which Mama Lena resorts to alter reality? Consider a couple of examples. When Walter Lee is suffering through the constant deferral of his dreams, he implores her, "I want so many things that they are driving me kind of crazy . . . Mama—look at me," with the clear intent of her seeing his pain. Rather than comply, she turns his anguish and his potential serious meaning in a superficial direction: "I'm looking at you. You a good-looking boy. You got a job, a nice wife, a fine boy and—" (60). Later, when the money is gone, she exaggerates the family's ability to make do in the space in which they currently live: "Been thinking 'bout some of the things we could do to fix this place up some. I seen a second-hand bureau over on Maxwell Street just the other day that could fit right there. . . . Would need some new handles on it and then a little varnish and then it look like something brand-new" (120). As Audre Lorde says her mother taught her, when you cannot change reality, change your attitude toward reality. Mama Lena can change reality on occasions, but she definitely changes her attitude toward it. These exaggerations and potential for changing reality thus raise questions about her relationship with Big Walter. How many women was he wild about? How frequently? And what kind of impact did infidelity have upon this strong black woman, in spite of her ability to contain it under her husband's ostensible love for his children? Whatever happened in the relationship with Big Walter, its relegation to memory now makes it pristine, and it makes Mama Lena's fidelity loom even larger.

In other words, by not showing any interest in men, Mama Lena is a *respectable* woman, so respectable that she does not even think of what it would mean to have a male companion/lover. And the setting of the play complicates that consideration. Where on earth would she and a man be intimate? While Hansberry allows for the modicum of privacy that Walter Lee and Ruth are able to have by allowing them a room to themselves, Mama Lena must share her room and bed with Beneatha, thus Hansberry has written out of the text any possibility for Mama Lena to have the privacy necessary to romantic relationships. By contrast, think again of Eva Peace in Morrison's *Sula*. Eva might be less than respectable by church ladies' estimations, but she refuses to deny her sensuality or her need for male companionship; even with one leg, she has several gentleman callers. For Mama Lena, the lack of consideration of the potential intimate/romantic part of her humanity merely places her more solidly into the self-sacrificial role of strong black women characters. Give up men. Give up sex. Give up privacy. Give up any thoughts of the flesh not immediately related to eating in preparation for work or feeling tired in response to work. Devote oneself exclusively to family. In exchange, earn the right to manage them with little course-changing objection.

Within as well as beyond her family, however, Mama Lena is a loner. That, too, is a serious consequence for the strong black woman character. As mostly undisputed head of her household, Mama Lena obviously has no peer. The hierarchy of power established within the family illustrates clearly that she has no one on earth to whom she can turn—even if she wanted to—for consultation about the decisions she makes. She might *look* "pleadingly" at her children and daughter-in-law on a couple of occasions to get them to *accept* her decisions, but she does not consult them in the decision-making process.

Her position and power leave her without a shoulder to cry on, without a designated sympathetic soul mate. On the first brief occasion when she seems to falter (when she admits that she has been wrong and helped to hurt Walter Lee as much as the larger society has hurt him), she even argues with him in taking blame. "I been wrong," she says, to which Walter Lee, probably sarcastically, responds: "Naw, you ain't never been wrong about nothing, Mama." Still going it alone, she retorts: "Listen to me, now. I say I been wrong, son" (86). On the second brief occasion when she appears to falter—after Walter Lee has lost the money—she still has no worldly soul confessor to whom she can take her burden. Instead, she adopts another directive posture and orders the family to begin unpacking the things they have packed in preparation for the move. Even when she is apparently "*lost, vague, trying to catch hold, to make some sense of her former command of the world*" (118), she does not share that lostness with anyone; she continues to make decisions in spite of her seemingly diminished state. True to one of the primary tenets of the strong black woman character, she keeps on keeping on, more alone than not. . . .

Finally, the psychological pain that Mama Lena inflicts upon others is also hers to bear. That is apparent in her reaction to Beneatha's disbelief, in Walter Lee's refusal to be the man Mama Lena envisioned concerning the proposed abortion, and in her disappointment when Walter Lee gives away the insurance money. Those scenes pale, however, in comparison to those in which she is strong and dominating. By sheer volume of representation, the emphasis is on the side of seeming psychological health, so that the minor rips in that tightly worn garment are quickly repaired. The tight reins that Mama Lena holds on her family only *almost* unravel in her hands. I emphasize almost here because the strong black woman character seems always to recover, and that is no less the case with Mama Lena.

She is *the* classic example of the problematic nature of the black female character's strength. Mama Lena was so well-received in 1959 precisely because blacks were more concerned about *inter*racial issues than *intra*racial issues. If a strong black woman character like Mama Lena could make the case for acceptability of all black people, then why quibble, as one of the reviewers asserted, over her excesses of characterization? The facts that she was on stage, recognizable, and representative were sufficient unto themselves.

Since Walter, Ruth, Beneatha, and Travis all seem to respect Mama Lena, another question arises. If her way of raising them is so troubling to close readers, and if she has such an insidious impact upon them, why is their response to her not more negative? I would argue that, in the mold of expectation and community imperative that governs Mama Lena's behavior, the same governs her children. They cannot ultimately reject the impact of her parenting because they are also drawn to reflect a particular time and place: the circle of acceptability that informs their historical counterparts also informs Hansberry's creation of them. The culture has taught them to respect Mama Lena, in spite of her tyranny, just as it has taught her to throw her weight around. But in terms of her impact upon them, imagine the other characters beyond the time frame of the play. Walter is probably still going to be dependent upon the women. Beneatha will probably become a doctor, perhaps more in spite of than because of Mama Lena. And Ruth is still going to be mousy. Travis is a question mark, but he has seen enough of how his family operates to know that women are dominant, men have little power, and his father has had to acquiesce to Mama Lena's wishes in order to win her approval.

The play-going audiences' acceptance of Mama Lena's excesses depended in large part on what I call a communal moral imperative. As I mentioned earlier, the general consensus was that the majority of "Negroes" at the time were religious, did not believe in abortion, were aware of if not acquiescent in various forms of domestic violence (especially in terms of parents disciplining children), and accepted all the foregoing as the norm. Indeed, this was a period in African American history that one could conceivably refer to "the black community," for—primarily due to racial positioning—views were more consistent than divergent. Consequently, black people joined with whites in finding the physically and religiously comforting image of Mama Lena acceptable in spite of her violence and invasions of privacy. As Ossie Davis pointed out, the mere fact that this recognizable black woman character made it to the stage satisfied just about everybody. Therefore, the average black person viewing the play, or for whom the play was written, probably did not pause very long—if at all—to meditate on the fact that Hansberry had joined with many white writers in portraying African American women, with slight modifications, in a particular stereotypical way. Her collaboration was just as effective as those earlier ones in which black actresses played the stereotyped roles assigned to them. Through Hansberry's tremendously effective portrayal, then, blacks and whites fell in love with Mama Lena, who, despite her tyranny, served as a source of comfort to both groups.

Notes

16. Other members of the cast appearing on stage and in the film included Sidney Poitier (Walter Lee), Diana Sands (Beneatha), Ruby Dee (Ruth), Glynn Turman (Travis), Louis Gossett (George Murchison), and Ivan Dixon (Asagai). Although Hansberry wrote two screenplays and new and substantially different scenes for the film, none of the new material was used. Carter points out that the film "was basically a shortened version of the play." Still, "the final product was good enough to earn a nomination for Best Screenplay of the Year from the Screenwriters Guild and a Special award at the Cannes Film Festival, both in 1961" ("Hansberry," p. 128). A second film version of the play, produced for television in 1989, featured Esther Rolle as Mama Lena Younger and Danny Glover as Walter Lee Younger; other cast members included Kim Yancy (Beneatha), Starletta DuPois (Ruth), and Kimble Joyner (Travis). The play was also transformed into a musical, *Raisin*, that appeared on Broadway in 1973 and has had many reprisals since then.

17. Lorraine Hansberry, *A Raisin in the Sun* (New York: Signet, 1966), p. 27, my emphasis. Notice that, although Hansberry emphasizes Mama Lena's beauty as much as she does her strength (in the sentences quoted and those immediately following), Mama Lena's beauty is never a factor in the play, while her physical and moral strength undergird most of the action.

18. "*A Raisin in the Sun* Revisited," 111.

19. Ferguson argues that Mama Lena's violence should "lead to an examination of African American views on corporal punishment—where such practice is not viewed as abusive and tyrannical but

corrective and loving. It's in the Christian tradition of violence as redemption. (Jesus hangs to save mankind.) Ruth uses the threat of a beating to keep Travis in line, too." Personal communication to the author, January 1997. From a different perspective than my own, therefore, Ferguson's comment connects nicely to the Christian basis for the actions of strong black women characters.

20. While it could be argued that the parent/child dynamic is reflective of 1950s historical black reality, in which children were expected to be "seen and not heard," that argument is flawed by the fact that, though she may treat them otherwise, both of Mama Lena's "children" are biologically—if not emotionally or economically—adults.

21. As many scholars have noted, Beneatha's very name places her in a lesser position, "beneath her," to Mama Lena.

22. In Raymond Andrews' *Rosiebelle Lee Wildcat Tennessee* (Athens: University of Georgia Press, 1980), the title character earns the appellation "the Momma" because of a comparable ability to meddle in everybody's business even as she cares for and nurtures them.

23. When Travis balks at going next door to borrow cleanser from a neighbor, for example, Mama Lena simply responds: "Do as you told" (53), which might be an acceptable directive to a child, but she treats the adults in her household the same way. When Ruth rises too soon from resting because of her pregnancy, Mama Lena asserts: "Who told you to get up" (54).

24. Particularly informative in this context are Sidney Poitier's comments on his discussions with Hansberry and Lloyd Richards about how the Walter Lee character should be played. Claudia McNeil was so strong as Mama, Poitier asserted, that unless the Walter Lee character were allowed to play directly against her, the play ran the risk of making "a negative comment on the black male"—presumably because he would appear weak. Poitier argued—and lost—that the play should unfold from Walter Lee's point of view, not Mama's. See Poitier, *This Life* (New York: Alfred A. Knopf, 1980), Chapter 17, "A Raisin in the Sun."

25. Ruth might not object overly much to Lena's actions because she has precious few other models for considering mature black womanhood. Remember that she threatens to beat Travis on a couple of occasions, an indication that she has perhaps been inadvertently influenced by Mama Lena. Keep in mind as well that she calls Mama Lena "Lena" or "Miss Lena." Is this an effort to identify, a desire to emulate—even though such aspirations might seem beyond the character traits we see in her?

32. A flaw in the play is the uncertainty about how much time has elapsed since Big Walter's death. The family seems ensconced and comfortable in its current relational and sleeping arrangements.

Where, for example, did Beneatha sleep before Big Walter died, since she is now in his place in bed with Mama Lena? Did Travis sleep in the room with his parents before Big Walter's death and Beneatha on the couch? How long did it take for the insurance check to be processed? Except for Mama Lena's acute memories of Big Walter at the moment of receiving the check, the family's grieving for its patriarch seems to be over. Clarity about these issues would enable more accurate interpretations of the impact of Mama Lena's sole influence on her family (e.g., how long she shaped Walter Lee by herself as opposed to raising him *with* Big Walter) as well as her obvious lack of interest in men.

GLENDA GILL ON THE PLAY'S 2004 BROADWAY REVIVAL

As two million black men languish in America's prisons, I believe that the casting of Sean Combs as the frustrated protagonist, Walter Lee Younger, in the 2004 Broadway production of Lorraine Hansberry's masterwork, *A Raisin in the Sun*, was unfortunate. In spite of Combs's extraordinary philanthropic work, he had few acting credits and very little formal training. The latter could also be said of Sidney Poitier, a relatively unknown actor at the time, who created the role in 1959. Today, however, there are a number of well-trained young black male actors with considerable acting experience. Since *A Raisin in the Sun* first exploded on the stage of the Ethel Barrymore Theatre, under the direction of the now legendary Lloyd Richards, it has repeatedly served as a vehicle for social change. Was this the goal of the director and producers of the 2004 production?

An assessment of Combs's controversial portrayal of Walter Lee Younger is impossible without knowing the historical background of such a major event. On 11 March 1959, audiences flocked to see the first Broadway production of *A Raisin in the Sun*. Sidney Poitier had the lead role of Walter Lee Younger, the husband, father, son, and brother who dreams that owning a liquor store will provide a way out of an economically depressed Chicago tenement dwelling. A stellar cast had been assembled including Ruby Dee as Ruth, the peacemaker wife, whose dreams are not clearly defined; Claudia McNeil as the strong-willed Mama Younger, who dreams of a decent home for her family; and Diana Sands as the dilettante feminist, Beneatha, the sister of Walter Lee, who dreams of becoming a physician. This was not an unrealistic goal for a black woman in 1959. But in all cases, these characters' dreams have been deferred and herein lies the tension of the play—four people in an emotional cauldron.

Langston Hughes's poem, "Dream Deferred," contains the crux of Hansberry's vision: "What happens to a dream deferred? Does it dry up like a raisin in the sun?"[3] While an explosive ending is clearly possible, the play builds to a crescendo of an unexpectedly happy ending. Walter Lee grows into his manhood as he quietly but firmly refuses to sell out to the white member of the "Welcoming Committee." "The play has been translated into over 30 languages on all continents, . . . and produced in such diverse countries as Czechoslovakia, England, France and the Soviet Union."[4] The universality of its message resonates with citizens of the world. Opening in 1959, *A Raisin in the Sun* ran on Broadway for 530 performances.

Ostensibly, the play is about an African American family on the South Side of Chicago. They live in a tenement dwelling in which the ten-year-old son sleeps on the couch and they share a common bath with the entire floor. Seeking to buy a home in a white neighborhood, Clybourne Park, where they are not wanted, they run into considerable resistance from a white community organization that tries to keep Blacks out. But the play is much, much more. It is about identity, self-respect, civil rights, the obsession with bourgeois values, fraternal relationships, marital relationships, racial pride/awareness, and parent-child relationships. Critics came in droves in 1959. Awards abounded including the New York Drama Critics' Circle Award. Excitement was electric. Woodie King, Jr. declared:

> From my standpoint as a resident of Detroit who had only recently become interested in theater and had no guide whatsoever, *A Raisin in the Sun* opened doors

within my consciousness that I never knew existed. There I was in Detroit's Cass Theatre, a young man who had never seen anywhere a black man (Walter Lee) express all the things I felt but never had the courage to express—and in a theater full of black and white people, no less![5]

It was a first for Broadway. Brooks Atkinson, dean of the New York drama critics, wrote of Poitier's portrayal of Walter Lee Younger: "Mr. Poitier is a remarkable actor with enormous power that is always under control. Cast as the restless son, he vividly communicates the tumult of a high-strung, young man. He is as eloquent when he has nothing to say as when he has a pungent line to speak. He can convey devious processes of thought as graphically as he can clown and dance."[6] Atkinson also called the play a "Negro Cherry Orchard" which critic Clive Barnes believes is an over-generous assessment.[7] Other critics compared the play to Arthur Miller's *Death of a Salesman* and Clifford Odets's *Waiting for Lefty*. Walter Kerr of the *New York Herald Tribune* declared, "There is nothing more moving in *A Raisin in the Sun* than the spectacle of Sidney Poitier biting his lip, clutching the back of a chair and turning himself into a man."[8] Kerr went on to praise Lorraine Hansberry for writing a play that captured:

the precise temperature of a race at that time in its history when it cannot retreat and cannot quite find the way to move forward. The mood is forty-nine parts anger and forty-nine parts control, with a very narrow escape hatch for the steam these abrasive contraries build up. Three generations stand poised, and crowded, on a detonating-cap.[9]

Amiri Baraka wrote: "For many of us it [*A Raisin in the Sun*] was—and remains—the quintessential civil rights drama."[10] Most critics and audiences believe *A Raisin in the Sun* to be as relevant today as it was in 1959. Did the director, Kenny Leon, of the 2004 production see this as a civil rights drama? ...

I am well aware that the 2004 Broadway casting of Sean Combs as Walter Lee Younger in *A Raisin in the Sun* excited the hip-hop generation as few things have done. At the same time, the casting antagonized a number of members of the older generation for whom Sidney Poitier's represented the definitive performance. The rapper cast as the protagonist in pursuit of the American dream mesmerized young America. If many of the young across America are like my students, they have little knowledge of lynching to which Mama refers in the play. They have limited knowledge of housing discrimination or any other kind. Walter Lee as the black chauffeur epitomized the black working class that in 1959 was still subject to formal segregation in the South and a more subtle form in the North. Walter Lee wants to buy a liquor store with the $10,000 of insurance money provided by the death of Walter Lee's father in an era when southern black domestics earned $12.00 a week. (Walter Lee is in Chicago, where his earnings as a black chauffeur may have been slightly higher.) Combs earns millions of dollars a year and despite his many philanthropic ventures, his image in his chauffeur-driven white stretch limousine is the antithesis of the character, Walter Lee.

Could Combs portray this role well? Elysa Gardner noted:

> The theater novice, who has acted in films such as *Monster's Ball* and *Made*, appears physically comfortable on stage and projects his character's emotions in a disciplined and expressive fashion. But projecting is not the same thing as acting, and the finely textured work of Combs' accomplished co-stars makes his own lack of experience and depth all too apparent.[13]

American youth bought his music, tapped their feet, quoted only the good reviews, and engaged in an orgy of worship of what some may call lowbrow culture. Combs's portrayal, according to some, made the play bridge generational differences. But does the hip-hop generation really feel Walter Lee's dilemma? Or are they only mesmerized by the beat of Combs's music when he is not playing the beleaguered Walter Lee?

Some critics, scholars, audiences, and directors believe the casting of Combs to be a sacrilege. I am among them. Is the struggle for money replacing the struggle for social justice? A well-known black theatre scholar living in New York City said he was staying home "on principle." He knew the production would be distasteful. Steven Winn of the *San Francisco Chronicle* wrote: "He [Combs] gets a hero's welcome from the juiced-up audience when he stumbles out of bed, the privilege and anticipation of a major star entering a new arena."[14] William C. Rhoden compares the excitement surrounding Combs's appearance to that normally accorded a sports hero. What does Combs, who now wishes to be called Diddy, represent? And is his representation one that affects all black men?

Walter Lee Younger is a walking time bomb, a caged panther who prances across the stage ready to pounce on his prey at any moment. One of many examples of Walter's justifiable rage comes when he physically threatens George Murchison, a member of the black bourgeoisie who is dating Walter Lee's sister, Beneatha. Walter Lee and Beneatha have just finished a "brave warrior" scene, complete with Beneatha's drumming and Walter Lee on the table top, shouting "That's my man, Kenyatta," while Beneatha urges him on with her drumming and chant of "Ocomogosiay, flaming spear." At the end of this "brave warrior" scene, Walter Lee, drunk and still on the kitchen table top, greets the snobbish African American, George Murchison, with "Black Brother" to which Murchison responds, "Black Brother, Hell!" (66).[15]

This important scene, representing the highly divisive class war between poor blacks and the black middle to upper classes, requires the skill of a seasoned actor who understands Walter's pain which is expressed more vividly than usual because of his drunkenness. (But this rage festers in his soul every waking moment.) Steven Winn observed: "Combs' sleepy stagger onstage at the Royale Theatre, it turns out, is unhappily prophetic."[16] Combs never seemed to have found the enormous range or rage required for such a demanding role.

As Murchison accuses Walter Lee of being bitter, Walter Lee responds, "Ain't you bitter man? Ain't you got no dreams you can't take hold of?" As Murchison exits the tenement dwelling for the theatre with Beneatha, he dares to taunt Walter Lee with "Good night, Prometheus," to which Walter Lee takes umbrage, not knowing who Prometheus is or if such a "person" even exists (72). This scene calls for considerable nuance and requires training in movement, as well. Diddy was judged not to have measured up to the task. Winn mercilessly continued his scrutiny of Combs: "In the splashiest legitimate stage crossover since Madonna's in David Mamet's *Speed-the-Plow*, Combs is probably making an even longer and more audacious stretch."[17] Milly Barranger writes: "The basic conflict in drama is not always solemn or tragic or loud, however. It may be extremely funny; or it may be muted and subtle. In fact, some dramatists, with the support of the psychologists, contend that our quietest moments are our most crucial."[18] Combs either lacked this knowledge or failed to show that he did. Projecting humor was also a challenge he failed to meet. . . .

An actor playing Walter Lee must be equally adept in shifting his mood from rage to laughter. For example, in one scene, he pokes fun at Beneatha as a militant, saying that he can envision her, as she begins surgery, asking a patient, "What are your views on civil rights, down there?" (93). Walter, in jest, says that Mama has not been very cooperative when, in a very light moment, the family chooses to give Mama gifts. Poitier literally danced around the chair in which Claudia McNeil sat. At the end of the play, Walter teases Beneatha that he is going to marry her off to George Murchison. Such humor can be missed or destroyed by an actor lacking the flexibility and range.

One of many powerful scenes in the play occurs when Walter Lee is considering Karl Lindner's offer to buy out the Youngers to keep them from moving into Clybourne Park. In an extremely poignant moment, Walter Lee, in anguish, says that he is going to get down on his black knees and put on a show for "the man." Walter Lee is embittered because he has lost $6,500 of the $10,000 insurance money in a get-rich-quick scheme. In a previous scene, when he learns of the loss, Walter Lee, in wild desperation, bemoans, "Not with that money, man, not with that money. That money was made with my father's flesh." Now more reflective, but clearly desperate for the money, he says, "Just give us the money and we won't come out there and dirty up your white folks' neighborhood" (124). These changes in tempo require an extremely supple performer. Steven Winn wrote:

> Time and dramatic momentum stop whenever the actor is called upon to summon Walter's impacted rage, doomed buoyancy and a final mustering of manhood. With his arms often dangling limply at his sides, his face frozen in a kind of pained blankness and his dialogue coming in an intelligible but uninflected blur, Combs wears the costumes and little more than that of his character. You can all but hear the whirr of his recently learned stagecraft, as he finds his marks, sets his body and unburdens himself of his lines.[19]

Walter Lee's buoyancy is not only seen in the "brave warrior" scene, but also in the scene with his son, Travis, as the play opens. He gives his young son 50 cents (which Ruth says they do not have) and another 50 cents to get fruit or take a taxi to school (19). In some versions of the play Walter Lee sees himself sitting down with Travis near him, allowing his son to choose any college he wishes. "Son, I will give you the world," he dreams. Walter Lee also gets so excited when the family decides, before Lindner's visit, to move into the new house. He and Ruth dance around the kitchen floor to a record Walter Lee has just put on the phonograph. Poitier played all of these scenes brilliantly, summoning a variety of gestures, body movements, and intonations. Combs did not muster these nuances. . . .

What, then, is a credible portrayal of Walter Lee Younger? Douglas Turner Ward believes, "Most interpretations of Walter Lee stress Walter Lee's 'becoming a man' at the play's climax, as he refuses to cravenly 'sell out' black integrity, legacy, values, etc. Inevitably, these analyses imply that . . . Walter Lee has been merely the repository of all the negative, materialistic aspirations of American society. . . ."[29] To Ward, Walter Lee is also "a complex, autonomous character who thinks and acts not as an author's marionette, but as harbinger of all the qualities of character that would soon explode into American reality and consciousness."[30] Walter Lee, in yet another example of the complexity, does not know his wife well enough to understand that she is considering an abortion. She does not have one but does consider one seriously, even honoring an appointment with an abortionist to whom she gives a $5.00 down payment. Walter can only think, "Ruth would not do that." Walter Lee and Ruth's highly strained marriage is caused by many factors.

According to Kalefa Sanneh:

> Like many other hip-hop stars, Mr. Combs seems inspired by the outsize legend and fearsome reputation of Donald Trump. . . . Combs more closely resembles Richard Branson, the peripatetic tycoon of the Virgin empire, who doesn't let his record company, his airlines or his cellphone venture quash his enthusiasm for adventure. . . . Mr. Combs is, if anything, more omnivorous: the dancer, record executive, producer and rapper is now also a fashion mogul (he runs Sean John), a former boyfriend of Jennifer Lopez, . . . a philanthropist, . . . and a marathoner.[31]

Is Combs, the man, so etched in the minds of America that they cannot see him as the character, Walter Lee, who turns down the money from Karl Lindner and settles for being a chauffeur? Sanneh continued, "As Walter, Mr. Combs will have a hard time persuading the audience to forget who he is; no matter how the scene is staged, he is likely to generate a laugh, when, in the middle of a money-hungry fever dream, he says, 'Rich people don't have to be flashy.'"[32] . . .

Given the American obsession with the almighty dollar, what happens to the image of black men in this country when Combs, however talented in so many ways other than as an actor, plays the role of Walter Lee Younger, a quintessentially classical role just as important as Willy Loman, Hamlet, or King Lear? In the annals of world theatre, in major theatrical venues, when we think of the casting of Hamlet, we think of Laurence Olivier or John Gielgud. When we think of Hickey, we think of Jason Robards, Jr. or Kevin Spacey or James Earl Jones. When we think of Willy Loman, we think of Dustin Hoffman. When we think of King Lear, Christopher Plummer or James Earl Jones comes to mind. Does Hansberry deserve less? Two million black men languish behind the bars of America's prisons, more than America's entire black male college population. Some of these men are completely innocent, some not guilty of violent crimes. Does such an extraordinarily rich black man as Combs numb white and black audiences to the reality of Walter Lee Youngers? The late Ossie Davis, who died 4 February 2005, wrote:

> Walter Lee Younger was a frustrated young black man whose dreams of better things for his family had been too long deferred and he was on the verge of exploding, either into crime or into revolution. Lorraine didn't say which, but she did imply that if America wanted racial peace, something drastic had to be done about the hundreds of thousands of Walter Lees all over this country.[39]

Sidney Poitier also had very strong opinions about how Walter Lee should be played:

> He could appear as a weak man overwhelmed by his mother—incapable of engineering his own life, which he has based on dreams that exceed his skills; in other words, a weakling who doesn't deserve very much attention. Or he could appear as the average man with an average potential and average dreams, who fails to achieve them only through a combination of misunderstandings in his own family and the racism of his environment—a man who winds up bested not because he is incapable but because circumstances conspire against him—a far cry from a weakling who is reaching beyond his grasp.[40]

Walter Lee is a man seeking dignity in a dignity-stripping world. Winona L. Fletcher cites Steven R. Carter's statement that Lorraine Hansberry's vision was that "an oppressive society will dehumanize and degenerate everyone involved."[41] Walter seeks acceptance in a materialistic and youth-oriented world where black men—especially—are measured by the size of their billfolds and their phalluses. Initially, Walter Lee tries to convince his mother that a liquor store is the way to invest the $10,000 his deceased father left the family. Failing to persuade her, he squanders the $6,500 his mother entrusts to him to put into the bank on a get-rich-quick scheme which blows up in his face when Bobo, "a man Travis [Walter Lee's 10-year-old son] would not have trusted" "skips" town. (111)

Clayton Riley suggests:

Walter Lee Younger's failure to convince his mother, sister and wife that wealth will provide details the play's most completely tragic element. For it is Walter Lee who wants desperately to slay dragons, in the basic and mythological sense, and it is Walter Lee's conflict—the test of wills between Walter Lee and his mother—that would be painfully dramatic even outside the racial context in which it appears in this work. Examined on the other side of fashionable dramaturgy about the black family, *Raisin* is a play about a mother and son who love but do not always like each other very much, and whose goals and aspirations are separated by more than just a generation gap. The familial ties holding the Youngers together have been frayed. . . .[42]

It is extremely difficult for a black man who is perceived of as the quintessentially rich black man in America to convince audiences that know his identity that he is a chauffeur.

Arguably, the end of the play presents the greatest challenge for an actor playing Walter Lee, when the character undergoes a metamorphosis and grows into his manhood. Refusing Lindner's offer to buy out the family, he completes a compellingly moving laundry list of why his is a proud family. Quietly, but spellbindingly, Walter Lee says: "This is my son, and he makes the sixth generation of our family in this country. And we have all thought about your offer—And we have decided to move into our house because my father—my father—he earned it brick by brick."[43] Sidney Poitier (in the film) virtually whispers most of this speech, concluding a performance that may well have been one of the most varied, intense, and nuanced performances given. Critic Ben Brantley writes that the 2004 revival "lacks the fully developed central performance from Mr. Combs that would hold the show together. This Walter Lee never appears to change, in big ways or small."[44] . . .

To many people who still long for the American dream, Walter Lee Younger is a strong black man who grows in the course of the play and achieves integrity. He has his flaws, but he overcomes the most prominent ones, cowardice and greed. Playwright Lonne Elder III wrote:

> In the final scenes of *Raisin*, the white Mr. Lindner comes to the Younger family's South Side Chicago apartment representing a white citizens' group from the lily-white community in which the black family has bought a new home. He offers the family a bribe if they will rescind their purchase of the home. Walter Lee, the oldest male in the Younger household, refuses the bribe in these simple but compelling words:

> What I mean is we come from people who had a lot of pride, I mean—we are very proud people. . . .[47]

To this, Elder adds:

> Lorraine had this to say in explaining Walter Lee's stance: The symbolism of moving into the new home is quite as small as it seems and quite as significant. For if there are no waving flags and marching songs at the barricades as Walter marches out with his little battalion, it is not because the battle lacks nobility. On the contrary, he has picked up in his way, still imperfect and wobbly in his

134

small view of human destiny, what I believe Arthur Miller once called "The golden thread of history." He becomes, in spite of those who are too intrigued with despair and hatred of man to see it, King Oedipus refusing to tear out his eyes but attacking the Oracle instead. . . .[48]

Walter Lee is a man who will survive in a world of literature along with Lopakhin, Faust, Othello, Oedipus, and Lear. He is no more nor less important.

Many African Americans and others feel that it is imperative that actors who play Walter Lee Younger, like those actors generally chosen to play historically white roles, bring with them the gravitas, training, and talent necessary to do justice to this major role. In a world of very mixed feelings about the casting of Combs, both audiences and critics have responded to his performance in very strong terms. A number, like Oprah Winfrey, applaud Diddy's courage. Others, including me, ask: In a world of strong, kind, intelligent, resourceful, considerate, talented, morally upright, and compassionate black men, can we afford, at this juncture, an actor of such questionable skills and credits in a drama of such cataclysmic proportions and import? A historic work that in 1959 promoted social justice in 2004 promoted the dollar. For me, the casting of Combs was an American tragedy.

Notes

3. Langston Hughes, "Dream Deferred" cited in the frontispiece of Lorraine Hansberry, *A Raisin In the Sun* (New York: Signet, 1958). All further quotations will be given in the text from this edition unless noted otherwise.

4. Jean Carey Bond, "Lorraine Hansberry: To Reclaim Her Legacy," *Freedomways* (Fourth Quarter, 1979): 183.

5. Woodie King Jr., "Lorraine Hansberry's Children: Black Artists and *A Raisin in the Sun,*" *Freedomways* (Fourth Quarter, 1979): 219.

6. Brooks Atkinson, "The Theatre: *A Raisin in the Sun,*" *New York Times*, March 12, 1959.

7. Clive Barnes, "Giddy for Diddy-Hop King and Talented Co-Stars Are Raisin' A Hit; Diddy's A Hit-Ty in Vibrant, Relevant *Raisin* Revival," *New York Post*, April 27, 2004.

8. Walter Kerr, "First Night Report," *New York Herald Tribune*, March 12, 1959.

9. Ibid.

10. Quoted from Amiri Baraka, "*A Raisin in the Sun*'s Enduring Passion," *Contemporary Literary Criticism* (Vol. 62): 239.

13. Elysa Gardner, "Sean Combs Not a Plum Choice for *Raisin in the Sun*," *USA Today*, April 27, 2004.

14. Steven Winn, *San Francisco Chronicle*, April 30, 2004.

15. Jomo Kenyatta (1889–1978) was an African politician who became the first Prime Minister (1963–1954, and President, 1964–1978) of independent Kenya. He was in prison in 1959, concluding a seven-year stay for allegedly organizing the Mau-Mau Rebellion.

16. Winn.

17. Ibid.

18. M. S. Barranger and Daniel B. Dodson, *Generations: An Introduction to Drama* (New York: Harcourt, Brace, Jovanovich, Inc., 1971), 3.

19. Winn.

29. Douglas Turner Ward, "Lorraine Hansberry and the Passion of Walter Lee," *Freedomways* (Fourth Quarter, 1979): 224.

30. Ibid.

31. Sanneh, 10.

32. Ibid.

39. Ossie Davis and Ruby Dee, *With Ossie and Ruby: In This Life Together* (New York: Morrow and Sons, 2001), 283.

40. Poitier, 236.

41. Winona L. Fletcher, review of Steven R. Carter's *Hansberry's Drama: Commitment Amid Complexity* (Urbana and Chicago: University of Illinois Press, 1991) in *Theatre Survey* 32.2 (November, 1991): 240.

42. Riley, 206.

43. Hansberry, 148.

44. Quoted in "P. Diddy Does B'Way, Reviews Mixed," accessed on April 27, 2004.

47. Lonne Elder III, "Lorraine Hansberry: Social Consciousness and the Will," *Freedomways* (Fourth Quarter 1979): 215.

48. Ibid., 215–16. Italics in original.

DIANA ADESOLA MAFE ON HANSBERRY AND NTOZAKE SHANGE

In her discussion of Lorraine Hansberry's *A Raisin in the Sun*, Margaret Wilkerson poses some pertinent questions about the 1959 Broadway hit: "What accounts for the extraordinary appeal of *A Raisin in the Sun*? How has it transcended the racial parochialism of American audiences?" (441). Similarly, Andrea Benton Rushing asks of Ntozake Shange's *for colored girls who have considered suicide/when the rainbow is enuf*, first performed in 1975, "What is there about this young and formerly unknown playwright's presentation of black women which has galvanized both black and white audiences?" (539). Such questions bring to light the remarkable and unanticipated success of Hansberry and Shange, two "young and formerly unknown playwright[s]" from different generations, and the "universal" appeal of their respective Broadway plays.[1] More importantly, however, these questions point to a broader inquiry where critically and commercially successful "minority" texts are concerned. How does a play about a lower-class black family or a play about "colored girls" become "universal," critically (ac)claimed by (white) hegemony as successful? Can these theatrical representations of "ethnic" culture be "authentic" if they are also read as "universal"? And, furthermore, what are the implications of hegemony reading these "ethnic" plays as exclusively representative of ethnicity? . . .

Both Hansberry and Shange address such controversial issues as abortion, sexuality, and female empowerment while challenging obstacles like sexism, patriarchal ideology, and gender stereotypes. But in their exploration of broader women's issues and feminist thought, these playwrights clearly write as/about/to black women. Their pioneering engagements with subjects like abortion or their representations of gender stereotypes must also be read in the "particular" context of black womanhood. By stressing female agency, self-definition, and the "right to choose," these plays posit constructive models of "universal" femininity. They also, however, signify important sites of black feminism in the larger socio-historic context of patriarchal civil rights and black nationalist movements, as well as exclusive white feminist movements. By striking these balances between the "universal" and the "particular," Hansberry and Shange ultimately manage to target a specific contingent (like the "colored girls" of Shange's title) but appeal to audiences across racial and gender lines—thus making history on Broadway and claiming a place in the literary trajectory of African American women's drama. . . .

Both Hansberry and Shange address such "universal" women's issues as abortion, sexuality, and self-empowerment from a black feminist stance, emphasizing the black woman's "right to choose." *Raisin* "is perhaps the first American play to address the issue of abortion" (Liddell 164) and one of the earliest plays to address racial pride, positive sexuality, and even atheism *through* the black woman. All of these issues are swept up in full force by Shange and made graphically explicit in the wake of the sexual revolution, the black power and women's rights movements, and the legalization of abortion that took place from the mid-1960s, to the mid-1970s. Clearly ahead of its time, *Raisin* serves as precursor and portent to *for colored girls*, teasing out the controversial issues that became markers of Shange's text.

Although the abortion in *Raisin* never occurs, the possibility of abortion remains not only a source of conflict for Ruth Younger, wife to the protagonist Walter Lee, but also an indication of her desperate yet no less valid agency as a woman.[7] As the female character with the least agency in the play, Ruth maintains her ostensibly natural "right to choose" whether or not to have an abortion, an extreme "prerogative" reminiscent of the black woman's agency during slavery.[8] In the face of her husband's hostility, a product of his own frantic search for agency, Ruth's threatened abortion confronts Walter Lee with the potential destruction of his progeny and simultaneously proves her ability to "take care of business." Initially, Ruth is unable to interrupt Walter Lee's incessant (male) speech long enough to inform him that she is pregnant, allowing her mother-in-law to convey the news of both pregnancy and impending abortion:

> MAMA: Son—do you know your wife is expecting another baby? (*Walter stands, stunned, and absorbs what his mother has said*) That's what she wanted to talk to you about. (*Walter sinks down into a chair*) This ain't for me to be telling—but you ought to know. (*She waits*) I

think Ruth is thinking 'bout getting rid of that child. (74–75)

When Walter Lee refuses to believe that Ruth "would do that," Ruth quickly enters the conversation to prove him wrong: "Yes I would too, Walter. (*Pause*) I gave her a five-dollar down payment" (75). Recalling that in the opening scene of the play, Ruth refuses to give their son Travis fifty cents for school because she simply "ain't got it" (28), we realize that the "five-dollar down payment" should not be taken lightly. Remarkably, Walter Lee cannot find a response to his wife's threatened abortion, despite his mother's outburst: "Your wife say she going to destroy your child. And I'm waiting to hear you talk like [your father] and say we a people who give children life, not who destroys them" (75). Walter's heavy silence and his immediate exit indicate a strange lack of male opposition. At various points in the play Walter raises a voice of dissent over other "female" concerns in the household, such as his sister Beneatha's college education or her interest in black nationalism, but in this instance he says nothing. Ruth thus enacts the complete *silencing* of Walter's masculine voice and finally exercises her "right to choose," ultimately choosing *not* to go through with the abortion. Unable to control the majority of events in a life of struggle, Ruth's choice is an example of her agency as a *woman* and her control over her own (female) body. In the context of the play, however, Ruth also represents the sheer desperation of a working-class black woman who literally cannot afford to have another child. . . .

Although Hansberry portrays Lena Younger as the stereotypical matriarch of the black family, a tower of spiritual strength, it is the youngest female character, Beneatha, who embodies the "new" black woman and prefigures the poetic women of Shange's drama. Lena admittedly constitutes a primary female force, but Beneatha represents the intellectual voice of feminist debate. Admittedly, Beneatha enjoys out-of-place middle-class luxuries despite the alleged poverty of the Younger family—marking a flaw in her characterization. However, her pursuit of play-acting, guitar lessons, and horseback riding, while decidedly impractical, clearly point to her search for a self-defined identity, something that her mother and sister-in-law (women of an older generation) find amusing:

> BENEATHA: —People have to express themselves one way or another.
> MAMA: What is it you want to express?
> BENEATHA (*Angrily*): Me! (Mama *and* Ruth *look at each other and burst into raucous laughter*) Don't worry—I don't expect you to understand. (48)

She eventually moves past her arguably white middle-class hobbies to locate a positive selfhood in her African heritage. In terms of a "new" form of black pride and nationalism, Beneatha embraces styles and fashions that later became popular in the sixties and seventies. More importantly, this character advocates West African music and dance in the play, artistic traditions that later became trademarks of Shange's choreopoetry.

Before cutting her straightened hair short and briefly adopting the Yoruba style of dress, Beneatha stands out in the play as an educated young woman who wishes to become a medical doctor, despite Walter's chauvinistic response: "Who the hell told you you had to become a doctor? If you so crazy 'bout messing 'round with sick people—then go be a nurse like other women—or just get married and be quiet" (38). Beneatha consistently rebuts the sexist male voices in the play, renouncing God along with other "assimilationist junk" (76) in her search for a self-defined identity.[9] She ultimately emerges (literally) in the play as a "new" woman, celebrating blackness and her African heritage:

> BENEATHA (*Emerging grandly from the doorway so that we can see her thoroughly robed in the costume Asagai brought*): You are looking at what a well-dressed Nigerian woman wears—(*She parades for Ruth, her hair completely hidden by the headdress, she is coquettishly fanning herself with an ornate oriental fan, mistakenly more like Butterfly than any*

Nigerian that ever was) Isn't it beautiful? (*She promenades to the radio and, with an arrogant flourish, turns off the good loud blues that is playing*). (76)

This passage, though illustrating Beneatha's newfound positive selfhood, also brings to light certain identifiable "shortcomings" in her portrayal. Beneatha expresses a flawed, essentialist notion of Nigerian culture, but is aligned with "Butterfly," a reference that indicates Beneatha's unconscious Orientalist performance of the submissive Asian woman. Beneatha further rejects "the good loud blues that is playing," an act that translates into a rejection of African American culture. Beneatha thus becomes the subject of debate and ridicule once her brother Walter and her date George Murchison enter the scene. Her empowerment, even her sexuality as a black woman, however, is not lost on the audience or the other characters:

GEORGE (*Looking at her*): You know something? I like it. It's sharp. I mean it really is. (*Helps her into her wrap*)
RUTH: Yes—I think so, too. (*She goes to the mirror and starts to clutch at her hair*) (86)

Regardless of this eventual approval, Beneatha consistently distances herself from stereotypes of womanhood in general and black womanhood in particular throughout the play, advocating her "right" to a positive self-defined image of female subjectivity. While contradictions remain in her characterization and the views she expresses, Beneatha represents a significant example for Shange's women, who also renounce a patriarchal conceptualization of God and instead find "her" in themselves (63).

The sensual, albeit fleeting image of Beneatha, a "colored girl," dancing a "folk dance" to a "Nigerian melody" is firmly incorporated into Shange's choreopoem, which relies on motions inspired by traditional West African dances to get the poetry across.[10] As Shange recalls of her choreographing history in the preface to the play, "Dance insisted that everything

African, everything halfway colloquial, a grimace, a strut, an arched back over a yawn, waz mine . . . The depth of my past waz made tangible to me in Sawyer's *Ananse*, a dance exploring the Diaspora to contemporary Senegalese music, pulling ancient trampled spirits out of present-tense Afro-American Dance" (xiii). In her poetic description of an emergent black woman, Shange takes self-definition, sexuality, and spirituality and moulds these concepts into a black woman's reclamation of "her stuff": "this is a woman's trip & i need my stuff / to ohh & ahh abt . . . now give me my stuff / i see ya hidin my laugh / & how i sit wif my legs open sometimes / to give my crotch some sunlight /. . . my rhythms and my voice" (49–50).

All the female characters in *for colored girls* eventually "mov[e] to the ends of their own rainbows" (64), transcending silence and suffering in their attainment of a positive and collective sense of "new" black womanhood that locates power in the female self: "i found god in myself / & i loved her / i loved her fiercely" (63). As Lester explains of Shange's rainbow metaphor, "The rainbow as a symbol works as a visual manifestation of women's spiritual beauty and eventual self-actualization. That a rainbow is not monochromatic by definition affirms the diversity of black females' experiences socially, culturally, and individually" (Lester, *Ntozake* 26).

Hansberry also employs a rainbow metaphor in her play, not for black women who have transcended suffering but for black men who have finally "come into their own." In the memorable final scene of *Raisin*, Walter Lee plans to accept money from Lindner, the sole white character, as payment for not moving into the white neighbourhood of Clybourne Park. Unable to go through with this act once Lindner appears, Walter Lee ends up affirming the worth of the Younger family and their right to move into any neighbourhood they choose. As the family literally starts moving out, Lena and Ruth have a quiet moment in which they acknowledge the realization of Walter's manhood:

MAMA (*Quietly, woman to woman*): He finally come into his manhood today, didn't he? Kind of like a rainbow after the rain . . .

RUTH (*Biting her lip lest her own pride explode in front of Mama*): Yes, Lena. (151)

This dialogue reminds the audience that Hansberry is also concerned with defining black masculinity, but it clearly situates the black woman as central to that defining process. Although Lena and Ruth do not address their own personal realizations as black women, the symbolic "moving up" to Clybourne Park speaks of Lena's agency in buying the home and Ruth's once again desperate agency in urging them to move when Lena decides that perhaps she "just aimed too high" (140): "I'll strap my baby on my back if I have to and scrub all the floors in America and wash all the sheets in America if I have to—but we got to MOVE! We got to get OUT OF HERE!!" (140).

The rainbow is thus equally, if not more appropriate for Hansberry's female characters, who have "come into their own" after tempestuous conflicts generated primarily by the male protagonist, Walter Lee. Consequently, when Shange writes, "& this is for colored girls who have considered suicide / but are movin to the ends of their own rainbows" (64), she encapsulates both Hansberry's female characters and her own, black women who have suffered, struggled, and considered desperate acts, but "finally come into [their] [wo]manhood . . . Kind of like a rainbow after the rain." If "[Shange's rainbow] represents discovered self-worth after a series of metaphorical storms" (Lester, *Ntozake* 26), then *Raisin* is truly a precursor to *for colored girls* as an earlier black feminist play which, though not for "colored girls," is certainly *about* "colored girls" for whom "the rainbow is enuf."

Operating specifically through black characters yet crossing boundaries of race and gender in the universality of those characters, *Raisin* and *for colored girls* celebrate the black woman. Having weathered such "metaphorical [and universal] storms" as "the death of children, 'necessary' abortions, and the exploitative actions of fickle, lying lovers" (King 122), these female characters find their agency in these trials. Hansberry and Shange locate the black woman's positive selfhood in her sexuality, spirituality, and pride, resisting stereotypes of both femininity and black womanhood. Ultimately, these African American women playwrights remind viewers that the "ethnic" is very much a part of the "universal." As Hansberry stated in a 1961 radio broadcast, "I don't think that there should be any over-extended attention to this question of what is or what isn't universal. . . . we don't notice the Englishness of a Shakespearean fool while we're being entertained and educated by his wisdom; the experience just happens" (Hansberry, "Negro" 92). Hansberry's comment remains relevant almost half a century later, urging audiences not to agonize over the parameters of the "universal" and the "ethnic," but instead to acknowledge the artistic value of these popular "minority" plays that strike such a fine balance between the two.

Notes

1. The link between these plays arguably originates in their respective statuses as the first and second play by a black woman to reach Broadway. As Brown-Guillory notes, "Seventeen years after the phenomenal run of *A Raisin in the Sun*, [Shange's *for colored girls*] rocked Broadway and touched the lives of blacks like no other before it" (*Their Place* 40).

7. I use the term "agency" circumspectly in this paper as a sign for both *conscious action* and *means*. Indeed, I suggest that the concepts of "threat" and "prerogative," which are central to my discussion of abortion, both constitute forms of agency.

8. My reference to abortion during slavery is not intended to be an exclusive example of the black woman's agency in that era. Both abortion and infanticide, however, remain haunting examples of black female agency, which merit acknowledgement and remembering.

9. Beneatha's claim that "there simply is no blasted God—there is only man" (51) is arguably problematic, although gendered language was standard when Hansberry wrote *Raisin*, which partially explains this seeming contradiction in Beneatha's feminist outlook.

10. Unlike Beneatha, however, who condemns blues as "assimilationist junk," Shange embraces both blues and jazz along with traditional African dance and music.

Works Cited

Bernstein, Robin. "Inventing a Fishbowl: White Supremacy and the Critical Reception of Lorraine Hansberry's *A Raisin in the Sun*." *Modern Drama* 42.1 (1999): 16–27.

Bhabha, Homi K. "Of Mimicry and Man: The Ambivalence of Colonial Discourse." *The Location of Culture*. London: Routledge, 1994. 85–92.

——. "The Other Question: Difference, Discrimination, and the Discourse of Colonialism." *Black British Cultural Studies: A Reader*. Ed. Houston A. Baker, Jr., Manthia Diawara, and Ruth H. Lindeborg. Chicago: U of Chicago P, 1996. 87–106.

Bigsby, C. W. E., ed. *The Black American Writer*. Volume I: Fiction. Baltimore: Penguin, 1969.

Bosch, Susanna A. *"Sturdy Black Bridges" on the American Stage. The Portrayal of Black Motherhood in Selected Plays by Contemporary African American Women Playwrights*. Frankfurt: Peter Lang GmbH, 1996.

Brown-Guillory, Elizabeth. "Black Women Playwrights: Exorcising Myths." *Phylon* 48.3 (1987): 229–39.

——. *Their Place on the Stage: Black Women Playwrights in America*. New York: Greenwood P, 1988.

Collins, Patricia Hill. *Black Feminist Thought: Knowledge, Consciousness, and the Politics of Empowerment*. New York: Routledge, 2000.

Fanon, Frantz. *Black Skin, White Masks*. Trans. Charles Lam Markmann. New York: Grove P, 1967.

Hansberry, Lorraine. *A Raisin in the Sun*. 1958. New York: Vintage Books, 1994.

——. "The Negro in American Culture." Bigsby 79–108.

——. *To Be Young, Gifted, and Black*. Ed. Robert Nemiroff. New York: NAL, 1970.

King, Lovalerie. "The Desire/Authority Nexus in Contemporary African American Women's Drama." Marsh-Lockets 113–30.

Lester, Neal A. "At the Heart of Shange's Feminism: An Interview." *Black American Literature Forum* 24.4 (1990): 717–30.

——. *Ntozake Shange: A Critical Study of the Plays*. New York: Garland, 1995.

——. "Shange's Men: *for colored girls* Revisited, and Movement Beyond." *African American Review* 26.2 (1992): 319–28.

Liddell, Janice Lee. "The Discourse of Intercourse: Sexuality and Eroticism in African American Women's Drama." Marsh-Lockett 155–72.

Lorde, Audre. "The Transformation of Silence into Language and Action." *Sister Outsider: Essays and Speeches by Audre Lorde*. Berkeley: The Crossing P, 1984. 40–44.

Lott, Eric. *Love and Theft: Blackface Minstrelsy and the American Working Class*. New York: Oxford UP, 1995.

Marsh-Lockett, Carol P., ed. *Black Women Playwrights: Visions on the American Stage*. New York: Garland, 1999.

McDowell, Deborah E. "Reading Family Matters." *Haunted Bodies.
Gender and Southern Texts.* Ed. Anne Goodwyn Jones and Susan V.
Donaldson. Charlottesville: UP of Virginia, 1997. 389–415.

Rushing, Andrea Benton. "For Colored Girls, Suicide or Struggle."
The Massachusetts Review 22 (1981): 539–50.

Shange, Ntozake. *for colored girls who have considered suicide/when the
rainbow is enuf* and *spell #7.* London: Methuen Drama, 1990.

Walker, Alice. *The Color Purple.* New York: Pocket Books, 1985.

Wiley, Catherine. Rev. of *for colored girls who have considered suicide
when the rainbow is enuf* and *spell #7,* by Ntozake Shange. *Theatre
Journal* 43.3 (1991): 381–83.

Wilkerson, Margaret B. "*A Raisin in the Sun*: Anniversary of an
American Classic." *Theatre Journal* 38.4 (1986): 441–52.

RACHELLE S. GOLD ON BENEATHA'S EDUCATION

This chapter takes as its point of departure [Amiri] Baraka's observation that Beneatha is able to climb the ladder of upward mobility "on the rungs of 'education' where [her family's] hard work has put her" (14). In other words, Mrs. Johnson, mouthing the sentiments of Booker T. Washington, may be right; "Education has spoiled" Beneatha, but perhaps not in the way that Mrs. Johnson envisions it has. Arguably, because Beneatha embodies many of the complexities that Hansberry desired to portray, audiences see Beneatha as a character to whom we are attracted, while at the same time, about whom we raise serious questions. As we admire her altruism in her desire to heal the sick, simultaneously, we puzzle over her self-centeredness to send her robe to the cleaners and to buy a fifty-five-dollar riding habit. As we value her commitment to expressing herself through activities such as guitar, photography, and drama, we wonder at her inability to dedicate herself to one hobby or her seeming inability to comprehend her family's finances. She is at a critical nexus between new modes of expressing herself as being a black woman that resist categories and old ways of expressing herself as a black woman that confine her. When she substitutes the values she learned in her internal home sphere with the cultural and ideological values that she learns in college, an external sphere, her family

146

finds her threatening. Compassionate and yet judgmental, she is both peripheral and central to the play's action. Her role juxtaposes the old and the new, and as a mixture of these two perspectives, she is complicated because of her paradoxical nature. Thus, the play introduces its audience to a corrupting element of education and engages the artistic and intellectual debate over the role of education in black communities.

Hansberry, too, some would argue, was spoiled by her education, some of which she received formally at the University of Wisconsin from 1948 to 1950, at the University of Guadalajara in 1949, and at Roosevelt University in 1950. She also learned less formally while studying art and writing at the New School for Social Research in the summer of 1950, as well as by studying African history and culture under W.E.B. Du Bois at the Jefferson School for Social Science in 1953 (Carter, 1991 viii). But Hansberry gained her political education, to a great extent, while working as a journalist for Paul Robeson's monthly newspaper *Freedom* from 1950 to 1953. Ben Keppel, in his book *The Work of Democracy: Ralph Bunche, Kenneth B. Clark, and Lorraine Hansberry and the Cultural Politics of Race* (1995), claims that "Hansberry spent her political and professional apprenticeship under FBI surveillance as an associate of Paul Robeson, the most known leader of the African-American left in the late 1940s and early 1950s" (179). Reared in a middle class home, Hansberry was influenced by her uncle, William Leo Hansberry, an Africanist at Howard University who introduced her to Robeson and Walter White when she was a young woman (Carter 8). Hansberry inherited a belief in the Du Boisian legacy of "The Talented Tenth" from her uncle and through her education, political activism, and artistry, made a distinctive contribution to the legacy in her own right. This is the educational and political background, then, that provides the back-story for the character who is to become Beneatha, modeled by Hansberry's own admission, after the playwright herself. . . .

Yet, Beneatha, as she appears to us in the play, seems a candidate unprepared to "elevate the mass." Throughout the play, Walter, Ruth, and Mama tease Beneatha about her distractibility and poke fun at her various suitors and hobbies. Despite her biology and African history classes, she has not yet put her education to any practical purpose. So, Mrs. Johnson's critique of Beneatha's educational pursuits seems quite understandable, "sometimes she act like ain't got time to pass the day with nobody ain't been to college. Oh—I ain't criticizing her none. It's just—you know how some of our young people gets when they get a little education" (102). An apt representative of Hansberry's vision that Negroes be portrayed in the theatre as "just as complicated as they [whites] are and just as mixed up" (63), Beneatha resists the simplistic categories that Mrs. Johnson's worldview affords, which allow her to be either a "good plow hand" or "one proud-acting bunch of colored folks" (103). However, instead of using the knowledge that she learns at college to assist her family, she uses her knowledge to insult her family members, to indulge her whimsical fancies, and to incite rifts within her family rather than to build bridges to understanding.

In writing Beneatha, Hansberry articulates a clearly expanded notion of not only a "new Negro," but also of a "new Woman." Indeed, Anne Cheney, in her book about Hansberry (1981), describes her in this way: "At twenty, Beneatha is very much the new woman: she is planning to become a doctor, she will delay marriage until she completes her training, she doubts God and various social institutions, and she toys with diverse forms of self-expression" (61). Also, Cheney offers an interpretation of her name: "Beneatha is an obvious pun, suggesting her contempt for many traditional ties" (61). Beneatha has opportunities open to her, namely education, delayed marriage to an educated man, professional autonomy and respect, economic advancement, sophisticated cultural entertainment, and international travel. In contrast, Ruth and Mama have not sought these opportunities, and while not openly hostile toward her, they realize that Beneatha has options that they have neither conceived of, nor imagined. Often, but not always, patient with her sassy sister-in-law, Ruth tries to keep Beneatha in her place by reinforcing the generational hierarchy. In the scene that ends with Mama slapping Beneatha, Ruth expresses dismay at Beneatha's ability to overstep boundaries: "Fresh—just fresh as salt, this girl!" (46).

Sharing Ruth's dismay, Mama, incredulous at Beneatha's announcement that she will be taking guitar lessons, asks "Lord, child, don't you know what to do with yourself? How long it going to be before you get tired of this now—like you got tired of that little play-acting group you joined last year? [. . .] I just wonders sometimes why you has to flit so from one thing to another all the time" (47). Clear-sighted, Mama has a true vision of who her daughter is, naming her fault openly, but Beneatha does not want to admit that she "flits." In fact, there is something to be said for the fact that she aspires to be a Renaissance woman, perhaps inheriting Mama's predilection for "aim[ing] too high" (139), who is accomplished in a variety of hobbies. Framed more positively, Beneatha may be cultivating a range of activities that will allow her to "pass" as middle class, and so she has chosen guitar and drama, because they do not strap the family financially as much as the equipment-intensive hobbies of photography and equestrian training did. By redefining her lack of commitment to any hobby as "expression," Beneatha condescendingly dismisses Mama and Ruth's laughter, with "Don't worry—I don't expect you to understand" (48). This dismissal reinforces the gap that Anne Cheney explains in this way:

> The old world of Lena and the new world of Beneatha are separated by more than forty years of social and political change. The old world looks inward to the kitchen, the family, the home; the new world stares outward at college, medical school, Africa. Since the Younger family is searching for a center, a nucleus, the old and new world cannot orbit peacefully: like stray neutrons, the two worlds were destined to collide. In *A Raisin in the Sun*, Lena and Beneatha clash—sometimes violently. (61)

Beneatha refuses to concede that Mama is right in assessing her lack of commitment as a fault, because doing so would be an admission of fickleness or an admission of the failure of that larger world in which she has been sojourning. If she admitted that her mother's evaluation was correct, she would diminish the knowledge that she privileges by claiming to be a member of the college elite. By this, I mean that Beneatha adopts the cultural values that she learns from college and is in the process of substituting some of her home values with the values that she is learning from this external institution.

Beneatha is, as we know, a first generation college student, and Mrs. Johnson's remark about the value of an education is noteworthy, especially when one considers that Hansberry herself was a student of W.E.B. Du Bois and is a product of his vision of "The Talented Tenth." But both Du Bois and Washington—although they differed greatly in terms of which educational curriculum black students should study and with regard to how black and white people should interact socially—agreed that the education should benefit one's family and oneself. Perhaps because of her youth, Beneatha neglects the responsibility that is part of the privilege of being the first to attend college, and instead of benefiting the family with her knowledge, she belittles them.

Beneatha uses two modes of knowledge to separate herself from her family, one where she merely broadcasts her beliefs, without asking anyone to subscribe to them, and one where she elevates her belief system over theirs, which highlights how Hansberry demonstrates the lack of "understanding" between the generations in the play. For example, after fighting with Beneatha in act 1, scene 1, Walter laments the servile attitude he must adopt at work, "Mama, I don't know if I can make you understand [. . .] You just don't understand, Mama, you just don't understand" (73–74). Beneatha, after telling Mama and Ruth why she wishes to have so many hobbies, exclaims, "Don't worry—I don't expect you to understand" (48) and later dismisses Ruth's inquiry about what kind of qualities a man needs to have to satisfy her, "You wouldn't begin to understand. Anybody who married Walter could not possibly understand" (49). Later in the scene, she explains her atheism: "Mama, you don't understand. It's all a matter of ideas, and God is just one idea I don't accept" (51). Mama is intensely aware of the gap as she intimately shares with Ruth after slapping Beneatha: "There's something come down between me and them that don't let us understand each other [. . .] the other done commence to talk about things I can't seem to understand in no form or fashion" (52). These scenes emphasize the rifts in understanding and show how being misunderstood is one of the major, but perhaps overlooked, themes in the play. . . .

Sometimes, however, Beneatha does share her view, in a neutral and inoffensive way. She merely tells her family how she feels, but the sense is that these ideas just exist. The knowledge seems innocently offered, rather than thrown in their faces. One might interpret her comments about her views on marriage, her awareness of birth control, and her assessment of Lindner in a very innocuous way and assume that she offers them in a spirit of show and tell—a "Here is what I learned at college today" type attitude. Keeping in mind notions of understanding and misunderstanding, Beneatha uses knowledge regarding six different topics, half of which are presented benevolently and half of which are presented antagonistically.

Telling and Showing: Beneatha's Broadcasts

First, in terms of her views of marriage, she questions not when, but "if" she will get married: "I'm not worried about who I'm going to marry yet—if I ever get married [. . .] —Oh, I probably will . . . but first I'm going to be a doctor" (50). Independent and headstrong, she rejects Asagai initially and questions whether she will get married, which was a nearly scandalous notion in 1959. Yet, when women were often economically dependent upon marriage, she still wishes to contemplate romantic relationships, for she believes, "there is more than one kind of feeling which can exist between a man and a woman" (62). Asagai counters with "No. Between a woman and a man there need be only one kind of feeling. I have that for you" (62). While she protests what she initially perceives as his lustful intentions, she refuses to merely accept what she thinks is a sexual proposal, defending her virtue by dismissing him: "I'm not interested in being someone's little episode in America" (63). Yet, at the same time, she allows herself to be smitten with Asagai's marriage proposal "Mama, Asagai asked me to marry him today and go to Africa— [. . .] (*Girlishly and unreasonably*) To go to Africa, Mama—be a doctor in Africa" (149–50). She wants to be able to flirt with notions of delaying marriage or avoiding it all together; yet, Ruth, Mama, and Asagai derail her notions of alternative types of relationships quickly.

Second, instead of expressing full joy and exuberance over Ruth's pregnancy, which would be a normal response, especially within the black folk community in 1959, she expresses shock, asks where the child is going to live, and is surprised that Ruth and Walter didn't "plan it" (58). By indicating that she understands the intricacies of birth control: "Did you plan it or was it an accident?" (58), she indirectly discloses to Mama and Ruth that she knows how to plan a pregnancy. Although the play is situated in a time before the pill and before *Roe v. Wade*, she knows how to avoid getting pregnant.

Third, she reads Karl Lindner accurately, but even as she offers her suspicions, both verbally and nonverbally, she conveys a sense of pride about the fact that she was the first one in the family to figure out that Lindner is not a benevolent neighbor. She is sassy and self-assured, showcasing her astuteness. When confronted with Lindner's explanation of what the Clybourne Park Improvement Association does, and before he offers the family money not to move there, the stage directions indicate that she "is watching the man carefully" (115). Later, after Lindner claims "that our Negro families are happier when they live in their own communities" (118), according to the directorial notes, Beneatha responds "with a grand and bitter gesture" uttering this ironic retort: "This, friends, is the Welcoming Committee!" (118). By this time, Ruth and Walter have figured out what Beneatha has already intuited. Lindner, trying to salvage the conversation, makes "A very generous offer" and an indignant Beneatha responds with "thirty pieces and not a coin less" (119).[5]

Beneatha's experiences dealing with middle-class white people at her college teach her to be more skeptical about what news Lindner could wish to share with the family on their home turf. Thus, the fact that she does not work as a domestic or a chauffeur, in this case, is an asset rather than a deficit, in that she has learned the ways that institutional racism can rear its ugly head and how to read between the lines for the rhetoric of bigotry, disguised as praise of racially segregated housing: "but you've got to admit that a man, right or wrong, has the right to have the neighborhood he lives in a certain kind of way" (117). Again, misunderstanding plays a central role in the scene. Lindner even tries to make overtures to solidarity by representing his community as "hard-working, honest people who don't have much but those little homes and a dream" (117). Interestingly, he is the one who feels misunderstood: "There is always somebody who is out to take advantage of people who don't always understand" (117), and after Walter tells him to leave, Lindner says, "Well—I don't understand why you people are reacting this way" (119). In this way, Beneatha's accurate suspicion of Lindner shows her skepticism of white institutions, but she does not demean her family, as the examples that follow show her doing.

Yelling and Shoving:
Inciting Political Gaps and Religious Rifts

Unlike the benign examples I just mentioned, some of Beneatha's remarks are made purposefully to divide her family and to highlight the rift between her belief systems and theirs. By showcasing her opinions, she is enforcing a separation between an "us" to which Beneatha belongs and a "them" to which the rest of the Youngers belong. Her intention with her remarks about George's family, her knowledge of Africa, and her proclamation of atheism are designed to elevate her status as the astute, worldly, and savvy one in a family of domestics and servants. Three examples show the ways in which Beneatha's knowledge incites rifts in her family that enforce a hierarchy between what she understands and what they understand about the world. It is her formal education that grants her knowledge about the class barriers in the United States, about her African identity and colonialism, and about atheism.

First, unlike Ruth and Mama, Beneatha is aware of the class barriers that exist in her relationship with George. In fact, Beneatha is shrewd enough to know that George is unlikely to marry her because she is from a different class; he is not downwardly mobile. Because Beneatha and her family are upwardly mobile, Ruth and Mama believe that George could help them as they rise from the ghetto; yet, Beneatha knows that George reaps no benefit in that equation. She clarifies:

> if the Youngers are sitting around waiting to see if their little Bennie is going to tie up the family with the Murchisons, they are wasting their time. [. . .] Besides, George's family wouldn't really like it. [. . .] The Murchisons are honest-to-God-real-live-rich colored people, and the only people in the world who are more snobbish than rich white people are rich colored people. I thought everybody knew that. (49–50)

Here is another way in which Beneatha subordinates her family's knowledge of the world and critiques what they understand by elevating the value of what she understands.

George agrees with Mrs. Johnson's perspective in that he envisions college not as a place to gain knowledge, but as an economic stepping stone to ease into the business world, completely disconnected from learning—which is the polar opposite from the way that Beneatha imagines it. This difference in collegiate expectations is related primarily to class in that George needs to jump through the hoop of college in order to inherit his father's business; his class position is stable. He desires greater wealth, but not greater knowledge. On the other hand, Beneatha thinks of college as a way to expand her mind, to express herself creatively, and to develop her ideas. When George, being brutally honest and tactless, tells her, "I don't go out with you to discuss the nature of 'quiet desperation' or to hear all about your thoughts—because the world will go on thinking what it thinks regardless" (96–97). Beneatha replies, "Then why read books? Why go to school?" George, who according to the directorial notes expresses "artificial patience" and then counts on his fingers, responds, "It's simple. You read books—to learn facts—to get grades—to pass the course—to get a degree. That's all—it has nothing to do with thoughts" (97).

Beneatha is stunned by this revelation and sees that the gap that separates her worldview from George's is nearly as wide as the gap that divides her from her family. Her views fit neither in George's upper-middle-class, bourgeoisie world, nor in her family's lower-class world; residing in a kind of no-man's land, Beneatha exists in a marginal space, not fully buying into the cultural values of the class to which she is supposed to aspire and not satisfied with the class to which she currently resides. It is as if the experience of college provides a bridge between the realm that she can claim and the realm that she dwells in; it is a kind of passing. Yet, despite the social lubricant of learning to speak correctly, and her adoption of middle-class avocations, she is not wholly comfortable in either realm. She rejects the shallowness, elitism, and superficiality of George's world and rejects the pat answers that religion provides to her mother; her family understands her aspirations, but not fully, for they may think that George can help her realize her dreams of becoming a doctor by providing her with the social class for which that profession will be a natural outgrowth. But they do not realize that he cannot satisfy her intellectually or emotionally.

After this clear articulation of how he understands the role of knowledge in his worldview, Beneatha has little to say beyond: "I see. Good night, George" (97). When her mother questions whether she had a nice time or not, Beneatha tells her she did not because "George is a fool—honest" (97), and Mama counters with "Well—I guess you better not waste your time with no fools" (98).[6] Before exiting to the room that they share, Beneatha looks at her mother and thanks her "for understanding me this time" (98) which implies, of course, that she often feels misunderstood.

Second, regarding Mama's knowledge of Africa being confined to Tarzan and saving people from heathenism, Beneatha treats her mother rudely and pleads with her, assuming she will embarrass her upon meeting Asagai, "Well, do me a favor and don't ask him a whole lot of ignorant questions about Africans. I mean do they wear clothes and all that— [. . .] I'm afraid they need more salvation from the British and the French" (57). Mama responds, intimating that her feelings have been hurt, "Well, now, I guess if you think we so ignorant 'round here maybe you shouldn't bring your friends here" (57). By insulting her mother's knowledge, Beneatha congratulates herself for what she knows about Africa, information that she prizes more highly than her mother's feelings or her mother's good intentions of donating money to the missionaries.

Third, when Mama and Beneatha are discussing her future professional plans, Mama tells Beneatha "'Course you going to be a doctor, honey, God willing." Beneatha replies that "God hasn't a thing to do with it" (50). Mama is shocked: Beneatha counters with "Well—neither is God. I get sick of hearing about God. [. . .] I'm just tired of hearing about God all the time. What has He got to do with anything? Does he pay tuition? [. . .] It's all a matter of ideas, and God is just one idea I don't accept. [. . .] There simply is no blasted God—there is only man and it is he who makes miracles!" (50–51). Beneatha's atheism is not homegrown; it must initiate as a result of her education. She imposes her college-influenced ideas about atheism on Mama and blasphemes in her mother's house in reference to her disbelief or skepticism about the existence of God. She should believe in God based on the way she was reared, but her collegiate experiences and readings in politics encourage her to question God's existence.

Beneatha bridges knowledge that she learns from college with knowledge that she learns from her status as a triple minority (poor, black, and female), and she is a force of incredible power, boldly expressing both her religious views and her civil rights values. Beneatha represents many anxieties that white audiences might have about the evolving type of Negro that she embodies. She is a budding feminist, educated, knowledgeable about her African heritage, skeptical about religion's role as a pacifying force, and sensitive to how class barriers restrict her from certain social relationships. She

156

seems to be a central character, yet is really rather marginal to the main plot. She is paradoxical on both structural and theoretical levels. Complex and charismatic, her position in the play is murky. She is loveable and frustrating, unimportant, yet pivotal. She is absolutely one of the most memorable characters, vital to the character development, and yet she is irrelevant and expendable to the main conflict in the play. Walter Lee losing the money to Willy Harris could easily be accomplished without Beneatha being in the play at all.

Notes

5. It is curious, here, to note that Beneatha, who claims "I don't believe in God. I don't even think about it" (51), would use a biblical allusion to Judas Iscariot selling Jesus to the Roman soldiers as the metaphorical reference to Lindner trying to buy her family out of moving into Clybourne Park.

6. Interestingly, Beneatha calls George a fool, and Mama agrees. In the omitted scene, Mama uses the same word to describe Booker T. when she talks to Mrs. Johnson.

Works Cited

Atkinson, Brooks. "The Theatre: 'A Raisin in the Sun.' Negro Drama Given at Ethel Barrymore." New York Times. March 12, 1959. 27.

Baraka, Amiri. "A Raisin in the Sun's Enduring Passion." In A Raisin in the Sun and The Sign in Sidney Brustein's Window. Ed. Robert Nemiroff. Expanded Twenty-Fifth Anniversary Edition. New York: Plume, 1987. 9–20.

Brown-Guillory, Elizabeth. "Black Women Playwrights: Exorcising Myths." Phylon 48.3 (3rd Quarter, 1987): 229–39.

Carter, Steven. Hansberry's Drama: Commitment and Complexity. Urbana and Chicago: University of Illinois Press, 1991.

Cheney, Anne. Lorraine Hansberry. Boston: Twayne Publishers, 1984.

Du Bois, W.E.B. "The Talented Tenth." The Negro Problem: A Series of Articles by Representative American Negroes of Today. New York: James Pott & Co., 1903.

Hansberry, Lorraine. A Raisin in the Sun and The Sign in Sidney Brustein's Window. Ed. Robert Nemiroff. Expanded Twenty-Fifth Anniversary Edition. New York: Plume, 1987.

———. "The Negro Writer and His Roots: Toward a New Romanticism." The Black Scholar: Journal of Black Studies and Research 12.2. (1981): 2–12. (First publication of a speech Hansberry delivered on March 1, 1959, at the American Society of African Culture.)

Harris, Trudier. *Saints, Sinners, Saviors: Strong Black Women in African American Literature*. New York: Palgrave, 2001.

Keppel, Ben. *The Work of Democracy: Ralph Bunche, Kenneth B. Clark, and Lorraine Hansberry and the Cultural Politics of Race*. Cambridge: Harvard University Press, 1995.

Nemiroff, Robert. (Adapted by) *To Be Young, Gifted and Black: A Portrait of Lorraine Hansberry in Her Own Words*. New York: Samuel French, Inc., 1971.

Robertson, Nan. "Dramatist against Odds." *New York Times*. March 8, 1959. X3.

Rodriguez, Richard. *Hunger of Memory: The Education of Richard Rodriguez*. New York: Bantam, 1982.

Works by Lorraine Hansberry

A Raisin in the Sun, 1959.

The Sign in Sidney Brustein's Window, 1965.

To Be Young, Gifted and Black, 1969.

Les Blancs: The Collected Last Plays of Lorraine Hansberry (includes *The Drinking Gourd* and *What Use Are Flowers*), ed. Robert Nemiroff, 1972.

Annotated Bibliography

Brown, Lloyd W. "Lorraine Hansberry as Ironist: A Reappraisal of *A Raisin in the Sun*." *Journal of Black Studies* 4, no. 3 (March 1974): 237–247.

Examines the play's complex portrayal of integration, racism, and the deprived dreams of black America.

Carter, Steven R. *Hansberry's Drama: Commitment Amid Complexity*. Urbana: University of Illinois Press, 1991.

Scholarly, comprehensive study of all of Hansberry's plays.

Cheney, Anne. *Lorraine Hansberry*. Boston: Twayne, 1984.

An in-depth study on Hansberry and her works. The chapter on *A Raisin in the Sun* provides an analysis of the play, with a focus on the female characters.

Domina, Lynn. *Understanding a Raisin in the Sun: A Student Casebook to Issues, Sources, and Historical Documents*. Westport, CT: Greenwood Press, 1998.

An interdisciplinary collection of commentary, with historical documents and references shedding light on the historical and social context of the play. Includes first-person accounts, magazine articles, excerpts from literature, and government documents.

Effiong, Philip Uko. "Realistic, Mythic, Idealistic: Hansberry and the African Image." From *In Search of a Model for African-American Drama*. Lanham, MD: University Press of America, 2000: 35–42.

Effiong studies the play's portrayal of the characters' complex relationship to Africa.

Gill, Glenda. "Techniques of Teaching Lorraine Hansberry: Liberation from Boredom." *Negro American Literature Forum* 8, no. 2 (Summer 1974): 93–95.

Discusses the importance of incorporating black literature into English classes. The author shares her success with teaching *A Raisin* and stresses the importance of student participation.

Gomez, Jewelle L. "Lorraine Hansberry: An Uncommon Warrior." From *Reading Black, Reading Feminist: A Critical Anthology*. Henry Louis Gates, Jr., ed. New York: Meridian Book, 1990.

A short essay that examines *A Raisin in the Sun* and the personal life of Hansberry and her activism.

Hansberry, Lorraine. *To Be Young, Gifted, and Black*. Adapted by Robert Nemiroff. New York: Signet, 1969.

A collection of Hansberry's writings and speeches that forms a loose autobiography.

Hannah, John M. "Signifying Raisin: Hansberry's *A Raisin in the Sun* and Wilson's *Fences*." From *Reading Contemporary African American Drama*. Trudier Harris, Ed. New York: Peter Lang, 2007: 153–181.

Examines the influence of Hansberry on the playwright August Wilson and how Hansberry affected the African-American dramatic tradition.

Harris, Trudier. "*A Raisin in the Sun*: The Strong Black Woman as Acceptable Tyrant." From *Saints, Sinners, Saviors: Strong Black Women in African American Literature*. New York: Palgrave, 2001: 21–39.

This work argues that Mama is a stereotype of a black matriarch yet also a powerful, memorable character.

Keppel, Ben. *The Work of Democracy: Ralph Bunche, Kenneth B. Clark, Lorraine Hansberry, and the Cultural Politics of Race*. Cambridge: Harvard University Press, 1995.

Focuses on the play as a social document of political radicalism and thematic complexity.

Keyssar, Helene. "Sounding the Rumble of Dreams Deferred: Lorraine Hansberry's *A Raisin in the Sun*." From *The Curtain and the Veil: Strategies in Black Drama*. New York: Burt Franklin, 1981: 113–146.

A detailed analysis of the play, with a powerful examination of the ending.

Kodat, Catherine Gunther. "Confusion in a Dream Deferred: Context and Culture in Teaching A Raisin in the Sun." *Studies in the Literary Imagination* 31, no. 1 (1998 Spring): 149–54.

Kodat examines the use of *A Raisin in the Sun* for teaching cultural studies. She describes how the play is useful for helping students think about literature within a historical context.

Mafe, Diana Adesola. "Black Women on Broadway: The Duality of Lorraine Hansberry's *A Raisin in the Sun* and Ntozake Shange's *For Colored Girls*," *American Drama* 15, no. 2 (Summer 2006): 30–47.

An analysis of *A Raisin in the Sun* and its presentation of strong female characters; also discusses Hansberry's influence on playwright Ntozake Shange.

McKissack, Patricia C., and Fredrick L. McKissack. *Young, Black, and Determined*. New York: Holiday House, 1998.

A biography of Hansberry, including photographs and a timeline.

Sinnott, Susan. *Lorraine Hansberry: Award-Winning Playwright and Civil Rights Activist*. Berkeley, CA: Conari Press, 1999.

Examines the life and work of this African-American playwright and social activist.

Stubbs, Mary Frances. "Lorraine Hansberry and Lillian Hellman: A Comparison of Social and Political Issues in Their Plays and Screen Adaptations." Thesis. Indiana University, 1991.

The thesis is a comparative thematic analysis of plays by Hellman and Hansberry, with a focus on social, political, and economic issues.

Wilkerson, Margaret B. "*A Raisin in the Sun*: Anniversary of an American Classic." *Theatre Journal* 38, no. 4 (December 1986): 441–452.

Discusses the strength and long-lasting impact of *A Raisin in the Sun*.

Contributors

Harold Bloom is Sterling Professor of the Humanities at Yale University. He is the author of 30 books, including *Shelley's Mythmaking*, *The Visionary Company*, *Blake's Apocalypse*, *Yeats*, *A Map of Misreading*, *Kabbalah and Criticism*, *Agon: Toward a Theory of Revisionism*, *The American Religion*, *The Western Canon*, and *Omens of Millennium: The Gnosis of Angels, Dreams, and Resurrection*. *The Anxiety of Influence* sets forth Professor Bloom's provocative theory of the literary relationships between the great writers and their predecessors. His most recent books include *Shakespeare: The Invention of the Human*, a 1998 National Book Award finalist, *How to Read and Why*, *Genius: A Mosaic of One Hundred Exemplary Creative Minds*, *Hamlet: Poem Unlimited*, *Where Shall Wisdom Be Found?*, and *Jesus and Yahweh: The Names Divine*. In 1999, Professor Bloom received the prestigious American Academy of Arts and Letters Gold Medal for Criticism. He has also received the International Prize of Catalonia, the Alfonso Reyes Prize of Mexico, and the Hans Christian Andersen Bicentennial Prize of Denmark.

Lloyd W. Brown was professor of comparative literature at the University of Southern California for many years before his recent retirement. He has written a book on Jane Austen's fiction; edited a collection of essays, *The Black Writer in Africa and the Americas* (1973); and edited the book *West Indian Poetry* (1978, 1984).

Helene Keyssar was professor in the communication department of the University of California at San Diego. Before that she had been chair of the dramatic arts department at Amherst College and had taught at Newark College of Engineering and Morris Brown College in Atlanta. During the 1980s, she pioneered interactive telecasts between the United States and the Soviet Union. She was the author of several books including *Robert Altman's America* and *Feminist Theatre*.

Margaret B. Wilkerson is emeritus professor of African American studies at the University of California, Berkeley.

Amiri Baraka is author of more than 40 books of essays, poems, drama, and music history and criticism and a revolutionary political activist. He is New Jersey's most recent poet laureate and acknowledged father of the historic Black Arts Movement.

Robin Bernstein is assistant professor of women, gender, and sexuality of history and literature at Harvard University. Bernstein's most recently edited book is *Cast Out: Queer Lives in Theater*.

Philip Uko Effiong is the author of *In Search of a Model for African-American Drama*.

Trudier Harris teaches at the University of North Carolina, Chapel Hill. She has lectured and published widely in her specialty areas of African-American literature and folklore. She is the author of many books including *From Mammies to Militants: Domestics in Black American Literature*; *Black Women in the Fiction of James Baldwin*; *Fiction and Folklore: The Novels of Toni Morrison*; *The Power of the Porch: The Storyteller's Craft in Zora Neale Hurston, Gloria Naylor, and Randall Kenan*; and *South of Tradition: Essays on African American Literature*.

Glenda Gill is a professor of drama at Michigan Technological University. She has published many articles on contemporary theater and drama.

Diana Adesola Mafe is a lecturer in the department of English and cultural studies at McMaster University in Ontario, Canada.

Rachelle S. Gold is a teaching assistant and Ph.D. student in culture, curriculum and change at the University of North Carolina, Chapel Hill, in the education department.

Acknowledgments

Lloyd W. Brown, "Lorraine Hansberry as Ironist: A Reappraisal of *A Raisin in the Sun*." From *Journal of Black Studies* 4, no. 3 (March 1974): 237–247. © Copyright 1974 by Sage Publications Inc. Journals. Reproduced with permission of Sage Publications Inc. Journals in the format other book via Copyright Clearance Center.

Mary Louise Anderson, "Black Matriarchy: Portrayals of Women in Three Plays." From *Negro American Literature Forum* 10, no. 3 (Autumn 1976): 93–95. © Copyright 1976 by *Black American Literature Forum*. Reproduced with permission of *Black American Literature Forum* in the format other book via Copyright Clearance Center.

Helene Keyssar, "Sounding the Rumble of Dreams Deferred: Lorraine Hansberry's *A Raisin in the Sun*." From *The Curtain and the Veil: Strategies in Black Drama*, 113–146. © 1981 by Burt Franklin & Co. Reprinted by permission.

Margaret B. Wilkerson, "The Sighted Eyes and Feeling Heart of Lorraine Hansberry." From *Black American Literature Forum* 17, no. 1: Black Theatre Issue (Spring 1983): 8–13. © Copyright 1983 by *Black American Literature Forum*. Reproduced with permission of *Black American Literature Forum* in the format other book via Copyright Clearance Center.

Amiri Baraka, "*A Raisin in the Sun's* Enduring Passion." From *A Raisin in the Sun and The Sign in Sidney Brustein's Window* by Lorraine Hansberry, Robert Nemiroff, ed. Originally appeared in *The Washington Post* (in a slightly different format). © 1986 by Amiri Baraka. Reprinted by permission.

Robin Bernstein, "Inventing a Fishbowl: White Supremacy and the Critical Reception of Lorraine Hansberry's *A Raisin in the*

their original publication with few or no editorial changes. In some cases, foreign language text has been removed from the original essay. Those interested in locating the original source will find the information cited above.

Index

Characters in literary works are indexed by first name (if any), followed by the name of the work in parentheses